GREEN CLEAN

GREEN CLEAN

Natural
solutions to
domestic
disasters

Shannon Lush &
Jennifer Fleming

EBURY
PRESS

1 3 5 7 9 10 8 6 4 2

This edition published for The Book People Ltd, Hall Wood Avenue,
Haydock, St Helens, WA11 9UL

First published in the UK in 2009 by Ebury Press, an imprint of Ebury Publishing

A Random House Group company

The Random House Group Limited Reg. No. 954009

Addresses for companies within the Random House Group can be found at
www.rbooks.co.uk

A CIP catalogue record for this book is available from the British Library

The Random House Group Limited supports The Forest Stewardship
Council (FSC), the leading international forest certification organisation.
All our titles that are printed on Greenpeace approved FSC certified paper
carry the FSC logo. Our paper procurement policy can be found at
www.rbooks.co.uk/environment

Mixed Sources
Product group from well-managed
forests and other controlled sources
www.fsc.org Cert no. TT-COC-2139
© 1996 Forest Stewardship Council

To buy books by your favourite authors and register for offers, visit
www.rbooks.co.uk

Printed and bound by CPI Mackays, Chatham ME5 8TD

ISBN 9780091932459

Illustrations by Ian Faulkner

NOTE

Every effort has been made to ensure that all information contained in this book is
correct and compatible with national standards at the time of publication. This book
is not intended to replace manufacturers' instructions in the use of their products –
always follow the safety guidelines. The authors and publisher assume no
responsibility for any injury, loss or damage caused or sustained as a consequence of
the use and application of the contents of this book.

CONTENTS

Introduction

Did you know that many common cleaning products contaminate the air you breathe in your home? How ironic, and horrifying, that in cleaning your home, you're actually making it unhealthy. Not only that, what about all those chemicals going down the drain and into our waterways? There are enough pollutants already – you don't want to add to them. The good news is it's really easy to change how you clean and the result will be a non-toxic home that sparkles.

Many people expect cleaning products to have overpowering smells because they think it means the products are more powerful. It's a mistaken belief that unless you're passing out from the fumes, you won't get rid of those nasty germs. But in making your whites whiter, you could be compromising your health when alternative products will do just as well without the toxic effect. It's particularly important if you have a baby or young children in your home because their little lungs are still developing.

Green Clean will show you what to stock in your cleaning kit and how to use your new non-toxic ingredients. Rather than chemical-filled cleaners, we use bicarbonate of soda and white vinegar to clean many surfaces – they're the staples of a non-toxic cleaning kit. Oil of cloves kills mould and lavender oil scents and removes many stains. Add antiseptic tea tree oil, eucalyptus oil, unprocessed wheat bran and good old-fashioned soap and you can clean just about anything in your home. We even show you how to use old tea bags to clean floors and kill dust mites. And throughout the book we give you techniques for using these ingredients correctly.

There's not just your health to consider but also cost and effectiveness. Sometimes manufacturers dress up basic products by describing soap and water with a foreign name, chemical name or abbreviation. In other cases, cleaning products contain unnecessary chemicals when basic soap and water will do the job. Many cleaning products claim to be all-purpose. But each stain has its own chemical make-up and its own solvent. Adding a range of chemicals changes the signature of the stain and can create further stains. Some chemical cleaners are so powerful they remove not only the stain, but the surface as well!

We challenge the view that non-toxic cleaners are not as effective. You may need to use more elbow grease but the results are just as good (if not better!), gentler on your health and less harmful to surfaces.

If you want to stop using smelly cleaning products filled with toxic chemicals, feel better about what goes down your drain, save money at the supermarket and have a sparkling home, this book is for you.

Stock your cleaning kit – it's time for some green cleaning.

CHAPTER 1:
Useful Ingredients and Essential Kit

I can't emphasise enough how important it is to have the right cleaning tools for the job. So here's a rundown of surfaces, useful ingredients and kit.

KNOWING YOUR SURFACES

When choosing a cleaning product, you have to know what the stain is and what surface you're working with. For instance, is your wooden table bare timber or does it have a polyurethane, shellac, varnish or acrylic finish? If you don't know, you need to find out. The same goes for any surface you're working with, be it fabric, vinyl, leather or even carpet. They all react in different ways to different products and cleaning utensils.

To work out what the surface has been sealed with, take a pin or needle, hold it in a pair of pliers and heat it on the stove. Touch the pin to an inconspicuous part of the table and smell the fume it creates. If it smells like burning plastic, it's polyurethane. If it smells like an electrical fire, it's an oil-based varnish. If it smells like burning hair it's shellac. If it smells like a snuffed candle, it's waxed.

Shellac, varnish and wax can be repaired using warm beeswax applied with the yellow side of a piece of lemon peel.

USEFUL INGREDIENTS

0000 steel wool is a very fine grade steel wool. Available from hardware shops.

Beeswax is the wax produced by bees when making honeycomb. It's a great polishing agent for sealed (except polyurethane) or unsealed wood finishes.

Bicarb (**sodium bicarbonate**) is a salt and an alkaline. It's also known as bicarbonate of soda, or bi-carb soda. Bicarb neutralises acid. During this process it releases carbon dioxide and water, which is great for penetrating stains or dissolving grease on many different surfaces. It's available at the supermarket, generally in the cake-baking rather than the cleaning aisle, and at chemists.

Blu-tack is a putty-like proprietary product used to adhere one surface to another temporarily. It can also be used to clean dirt from hard-to-reach areas.

Camphor is a ketone from the camphor laurel tree. It has a strong vapour that most insects, particularly moths, and cats don't like. It makes a great protector of gardens and wardrobes. It's very flammable so never heat it.

Carpet cleaner comes in many varieties. They can be soap-based, bicarb-based, detergent-based or alcohol-based. Be careful cleaning your carpets after they've been professionally steam cleaned because there can be adverse chemical reactions.

Chamois block a fine-grade cleaning block that is a very absorbent sponge, which removes moisture from carpet and other surfaces. Punch make one. There's an Australian product called Slurpex available at www.slurpex.com.au.

Cloves are a spice. They come from the dried flower bud of the clove tree. Oil can be extracted from them and used to inhibit mould. Cloves deter silverfish and moths and are great for cupboards and bookshelves.

Denture soaker can be used to clean and remove stubborn grey marks on porcelain. It can also clean craze marks on china and remove fruit and plant stains from terracotta.

Descaler removes rust, limescale and calcium deposits from kettles, coffee machines, steam irons, shower heads, toilets and sinks. It's available in various forms from the supermarket or hardware shops.

Epsom salts are hydrated magnesium sulphate and named because they were found at Epsom in Surrey. They are good as a bath soaker for aching limbs, for unshrinking jumpers and other woollens, and for magnesium-deficient plants.

Eucalyptus oil is an essential oil distilled from the leaves of certain eucalyptus trees. It's a paint stripper, adhesive solvent and also releases vapours that ease breathing and inhibit some pests. Unlike most oils, it mixes with water. It's available at the supermarket or chemists.

Fuller's Earth is high calcium clay with a mild bleaching effect. It's very absorbent. It acts as a wool relaxant and is used to unshrink or shrink woollens or remove sweat from felt or to block hats. It's available from chemists.

Goanna oil is an oil made from goanna fat. It's used as a lubricant and liniment and to restore glass that has glass cancer. It's difficult to find, but may be available from chemists.

Glycerine is an odourless, clear liquid. It's used as an agent in cosmetics, toothpaste and shampoos and is soluble in both water and alcohol. Glycerine helps loosen stains. It's available at the supermarket or chemist.

Graphite puffer is used to unstick locks and hinges. Graphite is a dry lubricant similar to a finely shaved lead pencil minus the clay. The puffer bulb allows access to tight areas.

Gumption is a whitish-grey cleaning paste that has many uses. It's great for cleaning baths and sinks. It contains a mild bleaching agent and abrasive. It's available from the supermarket.

Hydrogen peroxide is an oxidising liquid used as an antiseptic and bleaching agent. It's available at the supermarket or chemist.

Lavender oil is derived from lavender flowers and has many uses, including insect repellent, dog inhibitor, air freshener or toilet cleaner. Buy it at the supermarket, chemists or health food stores.

Leather dew is a combination of soap and oil and used to treat leather. It's available from shoe repair shops.

Lemon oil comes from the oil in a lemon peel and is used as a furniture polish, spider and insect inhibitor and stain remover, as well as for its fragrance and flavour.

Oil of cloves is cold-pressed oil from the dried flower buds of the clove tree. It's useful as a mould inhibitor, insecticide – particularly for silverfish – toothache soother and a cooking ingredient. It's available from chemists.

Plaster of Paris is a white powder made of calcium sulphate. It forms a paste when mixed with water and can be shaped before setting. It's also absorbent and good for removing stains from granite and pavers when applied in thick layers. It's available from art supply shops or hardware shops.

Rotten milk is formed by leaving milk in the sun until it forms into solids. The time taken to rot varies according to the weather and age of the milk. Rotten milk is great for removing inkstains.

Salt is an abrasive, a disinfectant and kills mould. When cleaning, use non-iodised table salt, coarse cooking salt or swimming pool salt, which are far more effective and cheaper.

Scotchgard is a fabric protector. It creates a water-impermeable coating to prevent spills and stains from penetrating fabrics without affecting the look or feel of the fabric.

Shellac is a varnish made from the resin secreted through the pores of the carapace of the *Coccus lacca* scale insect. This resin is then dissolved in alcohol or a similar solvent. It's used for making varnish, polish and sealing wax.

Soap (bar of soap) used for general cleaning. The only difference between the cheap and expensive ones is the perfumes, oils and moisturisers used in them. Cheap ones are fine for cleaning and often better.

Soap flakes are very thin pure flakes of soap. You can buy them as flakes or grate a bar of soap. You could also use a soap shaker for the same result. A soap shaker is a wire box with a handle. Place a bar of soap inside, clip it shut and run water through it or shake it in water to generate suds.

Soap powder is washing powder used for washing clothes in the washing machine.

Sugar soap is a highly caustic soap. It comes in powder or liquid form. The powder form is a mild abrasive.

Surex 002 Oxysure is a pool cleaning chemical and an alternative to chlorine. It kills algae, including mildew, and is great for cleaning paths.

Sweet almond oil is the oil from almond nuts. It's useful for cleaning bone and ivory and lubricating glass. It can be used to remove glass stoppers in decanters. Available from supermarkets and chemists.

Talcum powder is ground from a soft greenish-grey mineral. It's a super-fine abrasive, lubricant and is also very absorbent. It can be used for polishing, absorbing stains or soothing babies' bottoms. It also helps prevent rubber from perishing. I use talcum powder to determine the tracks of ants and fleas.

Tea unless specified, use black, Indian tea. Tea contains tannins, which are good for cleaning aluminium, killing dust mites and inhibiting insects. It's also a great pick-me-up when sipped!

Tea tree oil is an oil extracted from a tea tree bush and mixes with water. It's used as an insecticide, antibacterial, antifungal and solvent for resinous materials. It removes resin stains, such as sticky tape residue and wax.

Unibond PVA is a PVA wood glue and sealant. It's available from hardware shops.

Vanilla essence is the product of extract of vanilla beans combined with alcohol. It is used to provide fragrance and flavour to food and as a deodoriser. If you run out of perfume, dab behind your ears and you might get your neck nibbled! Available from supermarkets.

Vanish is a soaking agent that comes in several varieties. Vanish Oxi Action Crystal White removes some proteins, oils, organic or petrochemical stains, but can only be used if the item being cleaned is white. Vanish Oxi Action can be used on colours as well as whites and is good for tannin stains, protein, fats and oil stains. Vanish Pre-Wash is great for mystery stains and for underarm deodorant stains. Use Vanish as a soaker, powder or create a paste by adding water.

Vaseline is petroleum jelly that is used as a lubricant, a water barrier and to stop snails getting into your window boxes.

WD-40 stands for Water Displacement, 40th attempt. It's a high-grade penetrating oil and stops corrosion.

Wet-and-dry is a very fine (2000 grade) abrasive paper. Available from paint supply and car accessory shops.

Wheat bran is the ground husk of wheat or other grains. It's absorbent and can be used as a scourer. It is good for cleaning fabric, fur, silver or silver-plated items.

White vinegar is an acid. It's a preservative, condiment, beverage and, for our purposes, cleaner and sanitiser. Cider white vinegar can be used on hard surfaces that are not colour sensitive. Don't use it on white tiles, white laminex or anything that is lighter than the colour of the cider white vinegar. White vinegar is better for cleaning light-coloured surfaces. Both are available from the supermarket.

Witch-hazel is extracted from the bark and leaves of a shrub, *Hamamelis virginiana*: witch-hazel or spotted alder. Used as a soothing and mildly astringent and lotion. Available from supermarkets and chemists.

Woolwash is a mild soap combined with eucalyptus oil and bicarb of soda or detergent. As the name suggests, it can be useful in washing woollens when used in moderation. However I prefer to use cheap shampoo. Buy it from the supermarket.

THE CLEAN KIT

Brooms come in many varieties, including nylon, straw, copra, bristle and polycarbonate. Select the broom according to the surface and amount of soil to remove. As a general rule, the heavier the soiling, the tougher the broom required. They can be long-handled or short-handled. Nylon brooms have soft bristles and are best used inside the house. If you wrap an old T-shirt around the head of a long-handled nylon broom, it can also be used as a mop. Straw brooms are good for outside the house to sweep bulky dust and to collect cobwebs. Yard brooms have a wider head and are good for large areas such as driveways, paths, verandahs, garage floors and patios. If you can, clean the broom every time you use it. Do this by wetting a bar of soap with water then rubbing it over the broom bristles. Rinse the broom under warm water, shake the excess water off then stand the broom upwards to dry. Brooms are quite cheap these days so have several. You could even colour code them!

Buckets come in many shapes and colours. Square, oblong and round are the most common. Round buckets are either standard or nappy size. Choose ones with a pouring spout and lid. Use buckets to soak clothes, store washing water and transport items.

Clothes baskets aid the transport of clothes. They can be plastic, cane or wicker. Never have one bigger than you can lift when full. Plastic ones are light, come in a variety of colours and are easily cleaned with a little washing-up liquid on a damp cloth. Cane baskets are popular but wear more quickly, take less weight and, because they're unsealed, collect mould. Wicker baskets are rarely made any more but Shannon loves them because they last so long you can hand them down to your children. Wash them with salt water applied with a cloth every two months. When not in use, store all baskets upside down, so they don't collect dust.

Cloths come in many varieties, but the best cloth is an old cotton T-shirt or old cotton knickers with the gusset cut out. All are lint-free and can be washed in a washing machine on a hot setting. You can use proprietary cloths but there's no need to.

Clutter bucket is any kind of handled bucket used to transport items from one room to another. Select whichever size suits you best. I find allocating a particular colour for each family member is a good organisational approach.

Dusters I think the best duster is an old cotton T-shirt because it picks up dirt really well, is easy to wash out and won't scratch surfaces. Fluffy dusters tend to spread the dirt around the house so it just settles elsewhere. The best way to dust is to wipe a damp cloth over a surface. When we say damp, this means the cloth has been wrung out so tightly that it feels cool against your skin. If it's wet, you can feel the moisture, and the water will end up creating mud trails when you clean.

Dustpan and brush to collect dust, dirt, leaves and other items.

Elastic bands are used to secure items temporarily. They need to be strong enough for the job. We find they are mainly used to secure T-shirts over a broom head or vacuum cleaner.

Gloves can be disposable, rubber, cotton, gardening, polyurethane or acid-resistant. They protect the skin from chemicals, abrasion and heat, and can also help with grip.

A **hairdryer** is very useful for dusting, particularly delicate fine china. A hairdryer also helps to remove wax and can be used to apply heat to an area to speed up the drying process.

Mops can be made of rag or sponge, although newer ones combine the two and have spongy rags. I prefer to put an old T-shirt or pair of tights over a broom head and use that as a mop, because it's easier to clean and to clean with.

Old stockings are great cleaners and good non-scratch scourers, especially when cutting through soap scum. They're also handy to wrap around the backs of taps to clean. And they're cheap to buy if you don't have any old ones around the house.

Old toothbrushes – don't throw them away! Keep them to clean difficult-to-access areas, such as around taps and in tight corners.

Old T-shirts are great to use for mopping, dusting, polishing and wrapping over the vacuum cleaner head to protect surfaces. They're also very absorbent. If you don't have any old T-shirts, buy them at second-hand shops, which is cheaper than buying new sponges at the supermarket.

Paper towels are great for mopping up spills and clearing grease.

Rag bags can be used for storing old T-shirts, clothes, tea towels and towels to use as rags for cleaning. Old woollen jumpers are great furniture polishers. Just make sure you remove all buttons and recycle them in your button box. Make your own rag bag using an old pillowcase and simply attach it with hooks, tacks or screws to the inside of a cupboard or the back of a door.

Rubbish bags come in a variety of sizes, strengths and thicknesses. Whether you have tie tops or drawstring bags is your choice.

A **scrubbing brush** has a wooden or plastic top, and tough bristles. A washing-up brush, made of nylon or bristles, can be used as a scrubbing brush. Use on stubborn stains and in tight corners.

Sponges – use different coloured sponges so you don't contaminate your areas. I use green sponges on worktops, pink sponges on the floor and yellow and blue sponges in the bathroom. Wash sponges in a small bowl of half and half water and white vinegar, leave themovernight then rinse in hot water.

Spray bottles can be bought at the supermarket, or you can reuse an old spray bottle – buy the cheapest product that comes in a refillable spray bottle, use the product, clean the bottle in warm water then reuse. Check the bottle has a spray or mist option on the nozzle. Use removable labels and mark the bottle clearly. Spray bottles have many uses, for example, filled with lavender oil and water to use as an air freshener in the toilet.

A **squeegee** is a short-handled rubber-bladed implement used to wipe water from a surface. It operates like a windscreen wiper on a car. Use it to clean windows, the shower screen in the bathroom or to pick up dropped eggs from the kitchen floor. A squeegee can be bought at the supermarket, hardware or discount shop.

A **storage box** could be an old cardboard box, plastic box or wooden crate in a variety of shapes and sizes. Select one according to its use.

Vacuum cleaner sucks up dust and dirt from all manner of things using a variety of attachments.

How to use the vacuum cleaner

I get a great sense of satisfaction from vacuuming. I love it. But to do it properly, you need to know about your machine. Did you know there are other attachments for the vacuum cleaner? Find them inside the cover of the vacuum cleaner or in a separate bag. These other brushes and nozzles will change the way you vacuum. It'll be as though you had one hand tied behind your back all that time. These are the components of the vacuum cleaner and what they do.

❏   Barrel: This is the main part of the cleaner. It has an inlet and outlet connection. The inlet is where the hose goes. The outlet is where the air blows out of the machine and it's generally covered. You can attach the hose here to backflush. A leaf blower is simply a reverse vacuum cleaner.

- ❏ Bag: Located inside the barrel. Modern vacuum cleaners have a window that shows when the bag is full. If you don't have this, check the bag each time you use the cleaner. It's a good idea to change the bag regularly. The vacuum cleaner won't work efficiently if the bag is more than half full.
- ❏ Tube (hard part): Vary the length of the hard part to suit your height or according to what you're vacuuming. Make it shorter when vacuuming furnishings and longer when vacuuming floors. If you are tall, extra lengths are available from the vacuum cleaner shop.
- ❏ Tube (soft part): The hose connection.
- ❏ Main head: This can be set to have bristles up or down. Put the bristles down for shiny and hard floors. Put the bristles up for soft floors, unless you have pets. Clean any fur out of the bristles with a comb.

- ❏ Brush head: This small round attachment with long bristles is designed to clean cobwebs and the surface of furnishings, curtains and pelmets.
- ❏ Corner nozzle: Use this to access tiny spaces such as the sides of chairs, to clean around the buttons on padded furniture, or to get right into corners on skirting boards or into the grooves of sliding door tracks.

Work from the top of the room to the bottom of the room. Begin vacuuming with the brush head and remove cobwebs from the ceiling. Then clean the tops of things such as wardrobes, picture rails, dado rails, skirting boards, light fittings, window frames and sills and so on. Then change to the corner nozzle. Go around the skirting boards and floors vacuuming corners and edges. Then attach the main head and clean under furniture first then the main areas. Start in one corner of the room and move diagonally across. Vacuuming diagonally puts less stress on the carpet fibres and leaves fewer marks. Just before you finish vacuuming, spray and suck up some non-toxic insecticide into the cleaner to kill anything that might have landed in the bag.

If you're allergic to dust mites, suck a couple of damp tea bags into the vacuum cleaner bag before you start cleaning. And to send a gentle scent around your home without using an aerosol, place a couple of drops of lavender oil on a tissue and suck it into the vacuum cleaner before you start.

To find something small on the carpet, use your vacuum cleaner! Put a T-shirt between the head and the pole, vacuum the area and the item will stick to the T-shirt rather than going through to the bag. If you've dropped a packet of pins, needles or paper clips on the floor, attach a plastic magnetic strip across your broom or vacuum cleaner head with sticky tape. It'll pick them all up.

To clean the vacuum cleaner, vacuum inside the barrel and all the attachments, and clean the outside with a damp cloth. Wash the head in a mild solution of washing up liquid but make sure to dry it well so it doesn't rust.

CHAPTER 2:
Emergency
Action/Troubleshooting

When dealing with a stain, a lot of people think that they can improvise. After a spill, they head to the cleaning cupboard, pick what they believe might work, and give it a go. When that doesn't remove the stain, they try something else, then when that isn't successful, they bring out another product and on it goes until they end up making an even worse mess. Keep in mind that, every time you add another chemical, you change the stain's chemical signature. For example, if you spill red wine on the carpet, you can clean it with bicarb and white vinegar as described in this book; however, if you've mistakenly used soda water, then a spot remover, you can't then just use bicarb and white vinegar because the stain signature has altered. You're no longer dealing with a simple red wine spill – you have to remove the new stains you've created in addition to the red wine stain! The take-home message from this is: first, work out what the stain is, then what the surface is and fix it. Whoops! And What To Do Next...

WHOOPS! AND WHAT TO DO NEXT...

Here's a checklist of things to consider before tackling a stain.

Work out what the stain is made of – is it protein, fat, vegetable or mineral dye, pigment or resin/glue?

Know what the surface is – the kind of fabric, flooring, worktop etc. that you've stained.

Know the appropriate chemicals to use to remove the stain. If in doubt, speak to an expert. Try to minimise the number of chemicals you use.

Unless you know it will work, always do a test patch first. It's a good practice run!

Never spot-clean stains on your carpet within four weeks of it being steam cleaned. Vacuum the carpet four times before you spot-clean it as spot-cleaning stains can adversely react with steam cleaning chemicals.

Never use excessive water or moisture on carpet. More is not better!

Wear appropriate clothing, such as gloves, goggles and mask, if using any form of chemicals.

Don't make chemical mixes you don't understand. Mixing certain non-toxic chemicals can create toxic fumes. You could add one chemical to another and create a toxic fume, ruin a surface or even have an explosion!

Remove stains as soon as you notice them. Don't wait – they become harder to shift with time.

Stain-removal solutions are not interchangeable. You can't use advice relating to carpet on your woollen jumper. Every surface is different.

There is no substitution or approximation. If you don't know, get expert help.

HOW TO REMOVE BASIC STAINS

Protein stains are one of the trickiest to remove because you must not use heat, detergents or many commercial spot removal products on or near them. If you do, it sets the stain. It's just like cooking an egg, which goes hard as soon as you add heat. Many proprietary cleaning products will set protein stains. The best way to remove protein stains is with facial soap, cold water and, if it's on carpet, a little water. Scrub soap on the stain, then blot it with paper towel until it has been removed. Protein includes any animal product such as blood, gravy, meat, eggs, cheese and milk, and seeds and beans. Once you remove the protein part of the stain, you can then apply heat to remove other stains.

Oil, grease and fats include vegetable oil and butter. The best degreaser is washing-up liquid. You can see how it works when it's added to a greasy sink! Be aware that fat stains are often combined with protein stains. If food has been cooked in oil, or has fat in it, such as a lamb chop, the protein part of the stain has to be removed first. Make-up generally contains lots of oil too; washing up liquid is the solvent to use. The best way to determine oil stains is by rubbing the stain between your fingers – fat and oil make your skin slippery and shiny. To remove them, use washing up liquid and warm water. Only use the tiniest amount of water on carpet or upholstery.

Carbohydrates are starches and sugars. They're found in potato, rice and paper glues. The best way to deal with these stains is to allow them to dry, then brush or vacuum them out. For example, if you spill rice on the carpet, remove any solids, pat the area with paper towel, leave to dry then vacuum. If the stain has any other component, such as salt, dilute with a little water first, then apply the process described above. For sugar stains, add a little white vinegar or a little washing up liquid to help break them down.

Inks, paints and dyes require a solvent. Vegetable dyes, such as those found in naturally coloured foods, are best removed with sunshine. If you can't get the stain in the sun, use an ultraviolet light, which can be hired from the chemist. Sponge the area with a small amount of equal parts lemon juice and water, then aim the ultraviolet light over the stain. Check the stain every two hours until it fades. Some vegetable dyes oxidise, which means they respond to oxygen in the air – like a cut apple turning brown on its surface. As they oxidise, a tannin stain is produced. Remove tannin stains by wiping with a little glycerine, leave for fifteen minutes then sponge out with a cloth that's been wrung out in white vinegar. Repeat until the stain is gone. The glycerine takes the stain backwards in time a little. This procedure is particularly good for beetroot stains. Again, if the stain is on carpet, don't use too much moisture.

To remove **water-based paint stains**, remove with soap and water.

PREVENTION IS BETTER THAN CURE

It's a well-known phrase, but a good one. Though we can clean most stains, ask yourself before you embark on an activity: what can go wrong and how can I prevent it? Try to anticipate potential stains and put into place measures to avoid them. For example, for high dirt areas, spray carpet with Scotchgard (this works on shirts as well) and use old newspapers on the tops of cupboards to capture grease and grime. Don't do things like serve spaghetti bolognese on white shag-pile carpet – you're just asking for trouble! Create specific areas for doing messy jobs. For example, clean shoes outside or on several layers of newspaper.

And remember: when removing stains from carpet, always rinse chemicals out after you've cleaned. This applies even with basic chemicals, such as white vinegar and milk. If you don't, you'll be left with bad smells and more stains.

When doing the laundry, prevent disasters by reading the labels on your clothes. Use the recommended washing temperature. If the information isn't included on your clothes, I recommend washing in warm water – unless there's a protein stain. If there's a protein stain, wash in cold water. Warm water relaxes the fibres and makes cleaning easier. To avoid shrinkage, use the same water temperature in the wash and rinse water. Wash woollens in blood-heat water.

For new garments, put the iron on a cool setting in case the garment contains a fibre, such as elastin, that reacts with heat. You don't want to end up with a shrivelled shirt! Never iron clothes with any stains on them because you will set the stain.

QUICK GUIDE TO REMOVING STAINS

Below is a kind of ready reference or quick guide to stain removal from fabrics:

Banana   Wipe with a dab of glycerine and leave for 15 minutes, then wash normally.

Barbecue sauce   Wipe with a dab of white vinegar, wash normally and hang in sunshine to dry.

Beer (including lager)   Paint a paste of Vanish Oxi Action on the stain and leave for 15 minutes. Then wash normally.

Beetroot   Soak in white vinegar until the stain is removed, then wash normally.

Bird droppings   It depends on what the bird has eaten – either protein, seed or fruit. With protein (generally white poo), scribble over the stain with a cake of bathroom soap and cold water. With seed (generally black or brown poo), scribble over the stain with a cake of bathroom soap and warm water. With fruit (generally purple or orange poo), wipe with a dab of glycerine on a cloth and leave for 20 minutes, then wipe with a cloth dampened with white vinegar.

Blood   Rinse under cold water with a cake of bathroom soap and wash normally on the cold setting. If you can't put it through the wash, use a paste of cornflour and water to draw out the stain. Allow to dry and brush away. For old blood stains, use cold water and a cake of bathroom soap and vigorously rub the stain against itself.

Carrot Rub with a little white vinegar and hang in the sun. Carrot stains respond to UV rays.

Chewing gum Harden the gum with an ice-cube and cut as much off as possible with scissors or a blade. Then apply a cuople of drops of tea tree oil with a cotton ball, sprinkle over talcum powder and work the remaining gum out by rubbing it in circles.

Chilli sauce Wipe with white vinegar or lemon juice until most of the red colouring transfers to the cloth. To remove the oil, add a couple of drops of washing up liquid to your fingers and massage into the stain before washing normally.

Chocolate First clean with soap and cold water. Then clean with soap and warm water.

Chocolate ice-cream Clean with a cake of bathroom soap and cold water, rub with an old toothbrush and wash normally.

Coffee or tea For fresh stains, use glycerine applied with cotton wool, then wash in washing powder. For old stains, use glycerine, then dry-cleaning fluid and washing up liquid.

Collar grime Mix Vanish Oxi Action and water to form a paste the consistency of peanut butter. Apply to the stain and leave for 20 minutes. Wash and dry normally.

Cooking oil   Soak up as much oil as possible with paper towel. Apply a little dishwashing liquid and massage into the stain with your fingers. Rinse with a little water and apply more paper towel. Wash normally.

Crayon   Mix 2 drops of tea tree oil with 1 teaspoon of dishwashing liquid and massage over the crayon marks with your fingers, then rinse with water and wash normally.

Dog poo   Dip a cake of bathroom soap in cold water and scribble over the stain as though using a crayon, then rub.

Egg yolk   Rub with a cake of bathroom soap and cold water first, then rub with a couple of drops of washing up liquid and warm water.

Fruit juice   Rinse with white vinegar and hang in the sunshine to dry. UV light breaks down fruit colouring. For stone fruits and fruits with a high tannin level, treat the stain with glycerine first.

Gravy   Dip a cake of bathroom soap in cold water and scribble over the stain, rinse with cold water. Put a couple of drops of dishwashing liquid on your fingers and massage into the stain until it feels like jelly. Then wash normally.

Grease and oil   Apply washing up liquid to the stain and rub with your fingers to emulsify. Rinse under cold water.

Ink or ballpoint pen	Use rotten milk. Use glycerine first on red ink.
Mayonnaise	Massage a little washing up liquid into the stain with your fingers and wash in cold water. The massaging makes the mayonnaise water-soluble.
Milk	Wash normally on cold cycle.
Mud	For black mud, wash in the washing machine using a cold wash.
Rust	Use a descaler or lemon juice and salt.
Soft drinks	Treat as though it's a fruit stain because soft drink colourings are made of vegetable dyes.
Soy sauce	Wipe with white vinegar before washing normally.
Suntan lotion	Massage a little washing up liquid into the stain with your fingers, then wash with warm water.
Sweat	Make a paste of Vanish Oxi Action and water and leave on the stain for 15 minutes before washing normally.
Tomato sauce	Wipe with white vinegar and wash normally. Dry in sunshine.
Tumeric	Rub with a dab of lavender oil before washing normally.

Urine   Wash in washing powder and dry in sunshine.

Vomit   Cold wash normally and dry in sunshine or use *Vanish* if the stains are stubborn.

Watermelon   Quickly deteriorates and ferments causing a smell. Sponge with white vinegar and sprinkle with bicarb to remove the stain and the smell.

Wax   Place ice cubes in a plastic bag on the wax until the ice starts to melt. Scrape away as much wax as possible with a blunt knife, then iron between layers of paper towel until no more wax melts into the paper towel. If a small greasy mark is left behind sponge with a couple of drops of tea tree oil.

Wine   New red wine – absorb moisture with a paper towel, then wipe with a little white vinegar on a cloth.
Old red wine – wipe with a couple of drops of glycerine on a cloth, leave for 20 minutes and sprinkle with a little bicarb. It will turn grey. Sponge out with a little white vinegar, allow to dry and vacuum.
White wine – sponge with white vinegar on a cloth.

CHAPTER 3:
The Kitchen

The kitchen is the centre of the home. It's the room we gravitate to, particularly when we're hungry. Food is stored here, prepared here, served here and often eaten here. It's where the dirty plates and cutlery return, and where scraps and rubbish are dealt with.

I know it sounds obvious but, because food is stored and prepared in the kitchen, this is the most important room in the house to keep clean intensively and daily. Be vigilant about cleaning surfaces and floors. Any scrap of food, whether you can see it or not, will attract insects. Be guided by your nose because it's great at sniffing out any missed scraps – especially those dropped by children.

ASSEMBLE THE CLEAN KIT

bicarb – cleaning agent and absorbent
broom – to clean floors and walls
clutter bucket – to transport displaced items
damp cloth – to wipe over surfaces
detergent (washing up liquid) – cleaning agent
elastic band – to secure old T-shirt to broom head
glycerine – stain softener
lavender oil – fragrance
old stockings – to wipe over surfaces and behind taps
old toothbrush – to access tight corners
old T-shirt – to use as cleaning rag
paper towel – to wipe over surfaces
rags – to use as cleaning cloths
refuse sacks – to hold rubbish
sponge – to wipe over surfaces
spray bottle – to hold either white vinegar or water
storage box – to hold items
table salt – to deter cockroaches

vacuum cleaner – to vacuum floors
vanilla essence – fragrance and antibacterial
white vinegar – cleaning agent
washing-up brush – for washing up

CLEANING SPECIFIC TO THE KITCHEN

The best time to clean the kitchen is before doing the weekly shop because there's less food to work around. Begin by putting anything that doesn't belong in the kitchen into your clutter bucket. Once you've done this, leave the clutter bucket outside the kitchen. Items can be returned to their proper spots later on.

Clean the outside of the fridge, microwave, dishwasher and appliances with a sponge dampened with a little white vinegar. If you have grimy surfaces, add a little bicarb to the white vinegar cloth, but white vinegar should be enough to do the job. If there's staining on plastic surfaces, wipe with glycerine first.

Wipe the front of cupboard doors, the splashback and wipe the tops of canisters. Don't forget to wipe the range hood and to check the filter, particularly if you're using it a lot. If it's looking greasy, wash the filter according to the manufacturer's instructions.

OVEN

I can still picture my grandmother cleaning the oven. She used to wrap a tea towel over her face in an attempt to block the fumes created by the cleaning agent, caustic soda. It used to stink the kitchen out for a couple of hours. Methods aren't as drastic now, though I even prefer to use bicarb and white vinegar to clean the oven rather than proprietary products.

Be careful when cleaning ovens because most are made of enamel and steel. Enamel is essentially very tough glass fired onto a steel base and will scratch if you use abrasives and scourers. If you can, wipe the oven every time you use it and clean it properly every couple of uses. Just make sure it's cool enough that you don't burn yourself! Even if you haven't used the oven you should clean it. I know this sounds odd, but because it's a dark space, insects like to get inside. Remove the oven racks, rack supports, element and light cover, sprinkle the surface with bicarb, then spray an equal amount of white vinegar over the top. There will be a fizzing when the two come into contact. Scrub with a pair of tights or nylon brush as soon as this happens. To clean the sides of the oven, use one damp sponge dipped in bicarb, and another sponge dipped in white vinegar. Apply the bicarb sponge first, then place the white vinegar sponge over the top of the bicarb sponge and press the white vinegar through both sponges (known as the two-sponge technique). Once you've cleaned, rinse with water. If there are stubborn stains or burns, reapply the bicarb and white vinegar several times and use a nylon brush to scrub. Clean the oven glass in the same way. In order to see what you're cleaning on the oven roof, place a small mirror on the bottom of the oven.

Clean all the bits you removed with bicarb and white vinegar. For stubborn build-up, add bicarb directly to the nylon washing-up brush and scrub along the rack. If the build-up on the racks is really bad, use a plastic scourer. Never use a scourer inside the oven or you'll scratch it. Let them stand before washing in the sink with washing up liquid and water. Allow racks to dry then replace.

Clean the stove top by sprinkling with a little bicarb then spraying with white vinegar, wipe with a cloth, then rinse with a cloth wrung out in water. Gas rings should be removed and cleaned in water and a little washing up liquid. Make sure all the rings are clear and dry before putting them back. With electric stove tops, remove the elements and rings, then clean with bicarb and white vinegar. Make sure you don't allow the electric ports to get damp.

If you inherit a very scratched oven, sand it gently with damp 2000-grade wet-and-dry or have it re-enamelled.

 'I've got a huge scorch mark on the oven glass,' says Natalie. 'Is there anything I can do?'

Problem:	**Scorch marks on the oven glass.**
What to use:	**Bicarb, white vinegar, nylon brush.**
How to apply:	Sprinkle bicarb onto the scorch mark at about the same thickness as you would sprinkle icing sugar onto the top of a cake. Then splash it with an equal amount of white vinegar. While it's fizzing, rub it with a nylon brush, then rinse. You may need to repeat this a couple of times.

> **HINT**
>
> What is the two-sponge technique?
> The two-sponge technique is used to clean vertical surfaces. Wring one sponge out in water then dip it in a tray of bicarb. Wring another sponge in white vinegar. Place the bicarb sponge on the surface to be cleaned, then put the white vinegar sponge over the back of it and use your hand to push the two sponges together. This allows the white vinegar to mix with the bicarb and create the all-important cleaning fizz.

GRILL

A grill is really just a small oven and should be cleaned the same way. For day-to-day cleaning, take the removable parts of the grill out and wash with washing up liquid and water. Most stains should come off. For any stubborn stains, use bicarb and white vinegar as described for the oven.

HOB AND SPLASHBACK

I almost burned the house down when I was fourteen. I was making chips and answered the door. I was only gone for about two minutes and in that time the plastic on the extractor fan was in flames and the wiring in the brick wall was also alight. Never leave a frying pan cooking!

Wipe the area every time you use it with either bicarb and white vinegar or hot water and washing up liquid. Gas jets should be removed and cleaned in water and washing up liquid. Don't use a scourer because it will scratch the surface. Make sure all the jets are clear before putting them back.

Problem:	Smoke marks on splashback.
What to use:	Ash, bicarb, white vinegar, cloth.
How to apply:	Mix equal parts cigarette ash or ash from the fireplace with white vinegar and bicarb to create a slurry to paint over the smoke marks. Leave until it's almost dry and then wipe off with a cloth wrung out in white vinegar.

Problem:	Candle wax on hob.
What to use:	Ice cube, flat-bladed knife or plastic/wooden spatula, washing up liquid, cloth or old stockings.
How to apply:	Chill the wax by placing ice on it, then scrape as much of it away as possible with a flat-bladed knife. If you're removing wax from an enamel hob, use a plastic or wooden spatula. Then mix cold water and washing up liquid on a cloth to remove any remaining wax. You must use cold water because hot water will soften the wax, spread it and make it harder to remove. If there is any remaining wax that

won't scrape away, rub with a couple of drops of tea tree oil on an old pair of stockings or tights. If you are melting candle wax on the hob, use a double boiler and always heat and stir slowly.

Problem:	**Chocolate on the hob.**
What to use:	**Hairdryer, wet cloth.**
How to apply:	Always use a double boiler if you're cooking chocolate on the hob. Burnt chocolate sets like cement and can only be removed with a hairdryer and wet cloth. Lay the wet cloth over the chocolate. Then hold up one edge of the cloth and apply the hairdryer so that the chocolate melts into the cloth.

COOKER HOOD AND EXTRACTOR FAN

If you think about all the fumes and particles sucked up by the cooker hood, it's no wonder it needs to be cleaned. Most modern cooker hoods have stainless steel filters that can be put in the dishwasher or scrubbed in the sink with washing up liquid and a nylon brush. Use bicarb and white vinegar if the build-up is really stubborn. Charcoal filters should be washed backwards – that is, where the smoke comes out – and need to be replaced from time to time. Check the manufacturer's instructions. Using the extractor fan is the best way to minimise stains on cupboards and odours in your house.

The cupboard above the oven always ends up being greasy. Store canned goods here instead of plates or glasses that need to be washed to get all the grease off. And don't leave boxed goods here because heat and grease affect cardboard and can penetrate the packaging.

POTS AND PANS

Pots and pans can be made of stainless steel, aluminium, Teflon, enamel, copper, cast iron, tin or glass. The best way to wash them is with washing up liquid and water. Don't put pots and pans in the dishwasher if the handle is wooden, plastic or Bakelite because it will fade and crack. Stains will come off more easily if you put a small amount of water and a drop of white vinegar in your pots straight after using them.

If you have cast-iron pots, never put them in the dishwasher because they will rust. Instead, wash them by hand and dry them in the oven. Set the oven on its lowest temperature and allow it to warm, then turn it off and leave the cast-iron pot inside until it dries. Re-season cast iron with a little olive oil rubbed around the base with a paper towel, then let it heat through on the stove for a couple of minutes before wiping again with the same paper towel.

I have a very strong grip so I'm always breaking the plastic handle on lids. And there's nothing trickier than trying to remove a hot lid without a handle. An easy replacement is a brass or ceramic cupboard doorknob with a screw-and-nut back.

'I cook everything in my old wok,' says Graeme. 'It's got to the point that, if I can't cook something in the wok, I won't eat it! But it's accumulated all this build-up, which, despite some concerted scrubbing on my behalf, just won't shift. Is there anything I can do?'

Problem:	**Burnt pan.**
What to use:	**Bicarb, white vinegar, nylon brush.**
How to apply:	Sprinkle bicarb into the pan then sprinkle white vinegar over it. This will make it fizz. Scrub with a nylon brush while it's fizzing. You may need to repeat this two or three times for bad burns.

Problem:	**Egg stains in the pan.**
What to use:	**Eggshell, white vinegar.**
How to apply:	Place half an eggshell together with 240 ml of white vinegar into the stained saucepan. Leave for half an hour and the egg stain will wipe off. The reason this works is that the calcium in the eggshell leaves a chalky deposit that absorbs the egg.

Problem:	**Rust in the pot/pan.**
What to use:	**Potato, bicarb.**
How to apply:	Cut a potato in half and dip the cut surface in some bicarb. Rub it over the rust and then rinse the pot or pan in water. The starch and iodine in the potato remove the rust. The salt reacts with the starch and iodine and forms a mild caustic.

Problem:	**Dent in a pan.**
What to use:	**Wooden spoon, hammer.**
How to apply:	Place the edge of a wooden spoon on the pointed side of the dent, then tap a hammer lightly onto the other edge of the wooden spoon until the dent smoothes out. If the bottom of the pan has a dent, place one block inside and another block underneath the pan, then hammer the blocks and it will smooth out so you can cook evenly again. This technique can also be used for Teflon pans.

Q: 'I picked up some old Bakelite canisters at a second-hand shop,' says Jane, 'but they've got some scratches on them. Is there anything to be done?'

Problem:	**Scratches in old Bakelite canisters/handles.**
What to use:	**Sweet almond oil, paper towel.**
How to apply:	Apply a small quantity of sweet almond oil with a paper towel or cotton wool ball. Then wipe it off.

Problem:	**A glued pot handle has cracked and come loose.**
What to use:	**Butcher's twine, heat-resistant superglue.**
How to apply:	Strap the handle with butcher's twine then cover the strapped handle with heat-resistant superglue. This forms a seal that is hygienic and non-toxic. It can loosen again if washed repeatedly in a dishwasher or if it's left soaking in boiling water.

APPLIANCES

Whether it's grinding coffee or making bread, there's an appliance for everything. Most appliances can be cleaned with washing up liquid and water either in the sink or with a sponge. Clean them as soon as you can because, when food sets, it becomes much more difficult to remove. Pull the appliance apart as much as possible, but never put electrics in water. If there's staining on plastic surfaces, wipe with glycerine first, then use bicarb and white vinegar. To remove rust marks on plastic, use a paste of glycerine and talcum powder.

Kettle

I drink massive amounts of tea every day so I'm very used to
cleaning the kettle. For general cleaning on the outside, use bicarb
and white vinegar. Apply with two sponges, one with bicarb on it,
the other with white vinegar on it. Start with the bicarb sponge then
rub the white vinegar sponge over the surface.

Q: 'My stainless-steel electric kettle has a build up of
gunk from years of use,' says Cecily. 'What should
I do?'

Problem:	**Scaling in the kettle.**
What to use:	**Uncooked white rice, bicarb, white vinegar.**
How to apply:	Place 2 tablespoons each of uncooked white rice, bicarb and white vinegar into the kettle, with your hands over the spout and lid, and shake. The uncooked rice acts as a scourer getting into those places you can't reach. Rinse out with water thoroughly afterwards. Make sure you clean it out well or your next cup of tea will taste a bit funny.

Espresso/coffee machines

Clean with bicarb and white vinegar. Any areas that have contact
with coffee should then be rinsed with a salt solution, which also
makes the coffee taste better. The areas that come into contact with
milk need to be cleaned with cold water first to remove proteins
and then cleaned with hot water to remove fats. It's not a good idea
to use washing up liquid because it curdles milk and makes the
curds stick to the surface, encouraging bacterial growth.

Mixers and blenders

Clean the inside of blenders by adding 2 teaspoons of bicarb and 120 ml of white vinegar and then switching the blender on. Make sure you cover the blender first or you'll be cleaning the whole kitchen. Then rinse out with water. If you're blending anything hot, place a clean tea towel over the blender before you put the lid on. It protects the plastic in the lid from melting, stretching or shrinking and will lessen mess in the kitchen if the lid takes off because of too much heat inside. If the fit is poor, hold the lid with your hand while blending.

Toaster

Clean the outside of a toaster with bicarb on one sponge and white vinegar on another sponge. Wipe with the bicarb sponge first, then the white vinegar sponge. For the interior, sprinkle coarse salt in the top of the toaster, cover the slots with your hand and shake it up and down a few times. This cleans it and helps prevent vermin. When you've finished, shake the contents into the bin. Make sure you get all the salt out or it may cause corrosion.

How to get stains off an old thermos

To clean an old stained flask or thermos, put 2 teaspoons of bicarb and 120 ml of white vinegar inside. Put the lid on and give it a shake, but not for too long or it will explode. Take the lid off, let it sit for half an hour, top it up with hot water and leave overnight. The next morning, give it a shake and rinse.

Microwave

I love the microwave and it's much easier to clean than the oven. The glass or china turntable can be removed and cleaned in the sink with washing up liquid. Make sure it's dry before you replace it or your rollers will rust. Remove the nylon turning ring and wheels and clean in washing up liquid, then dry them.

For the interior, sprinkle bicarb over first, then add white vinegar and wipe with a sponge. For the sides and top, use the two-sponge method: wipe with the bicarb one first, then the white vinegar one.

Check the inside of the microwave. Ideally, you should clean the inside of the microwave as soon as any mess is made, but if you haven't, do it now. If old food is caked on, mix 120 ml white vinegar, 240 ml of water and 1 tablespoon of bicarb in a large microwave-safe bowl. Put the bowl in the microwave without a lid and cook on high. The amount of time you leave it cooking will depend on the strength of your microwave. Allow the mixture to boil, but not boil over, for around 1 minute. While it's warm and steamy, wipe the interior with a cloth dipped in the solution.

Problem:	**Food splattered inside the microwave.**
What to use:	**White vinegar, water, bicarb, large microwave-proof bowl.**
How to apply:	Mix 120 ml of white vinegar, 240 ml of water and 1 tablespoon of bicarb in a large bowl. Put the bowl in the microwave without a lid on and cook on high for a few minutes, allowing the mixture to boil, but not boil over, for around 1 minute. While the microwave is warm and steamy, wipe the interior down with a cloth dipped in the solution.

Dishwasher

Dishwashers may have saved many relationships, but they've ruined plenty of crockery, cutlery and glassware. I hate them, because dishwashers clean by flinging small particles of soap, food and water at high speed, which virtually sandblasts your plates and cutlery. Bear this in mind when putting things in – never put fine china, crystal, items with gold edging or good cutlery in the dishwasher. Some of the damage won't be fixable, even by me. For other items, always rinse before putting them in. Heat-sensitive items should sit at the top; saucepans should sit at an angle towards the bottom centre of the dishwasher. And don't overpack the dishwasher because china and glass can break if they bang together. Don't put electrical parts in. Even if you always use a good quality soap and rinse agent that dissolves well, the high caustic nature of dishwasher soaps can cause gradual damage to the objects that you put inside. An alternative washing agent is bicarb rather than soap and white vinegar instead of rinse aid.

If your dishwasher has an odour, put bicarb in the detergent compartment and white vinegar in the rinse-aid compartment and turn the dishwasher on for an empty run. This will clean the drainpipes at the same time. If the dishwasher really stinks, wipe the rubbers and interiors with vanilla essence. This removes the smell and acts as an antibacterial. If the rubbers become perished, they harbour bacteria. To help prevent perishing, rub the surfaces with dry salt and then vanilla essence.

Clean inside the dishwasher once a week with bicarb and white vinegar using the two-sponge technique. To stop the plumbing from becoming corroded, run the dishwasher empty once a week with bicarb in the soap compartment and white vinegar in the rinse aid compartment. Remove and clean the filter at the bottom of the dishwasher.

If you have cockroaches, make sure they don't get inside the front of the dishwasher and into the liquid crystal display because it can short the dishwasher. To stop them getting in, wipe around the seals of the dishwasher with a cloth wrung out in table salt and water. Keep the kitchen free of crumbs and other cockroach food supplies. Alternatively, you can spray the surrounds, but not the interior, of the dishwasher with insecticide.

How to stack and unstack the dishwasher speedily
Always rinse off any food before putting items in the dishwasher. To speed your stacking, put like items, such as plates, together. Put matching cutlery in the same compartment, so all knives, for example, sit together. It makes unstacking quicker.

After you've stacked the dishwasher, check that the propeller in the middle of the machine can spin freely so that water spreads throughout the interior. Also check that the spray jets are clear and avoid the embarrassment that a friend of mine had when she received a lecture from a repairman for allowing her jets to clog. Have the top shelf raised or lowered to suit the size of your plates. This will make using it speedier.

Refrigerator

I'll never forget the state of my friend's fridge when I helped him move house. It had been switched off for a few weeks and the door had been left closed tightly. When we opened it, mould had grown all the way to the door and filled every cavity. We ended up hosing it clean in the garden.

Most fridges are easy to look after, especially those with auto-defrost. Clean the fridge once a month with bicarb and white vinegar. The best time to clean is just before you do your shopping because it'll be fairly empty. Pull the shelves and compartments out and wash them with bicarb and white vinegar. To clean the sides of the fridge, put bicarb on one sponge and white vinegar on another and press the white vinegar sponge through the bicarb sponge when cleaning.

To cut back on cleaning, put a thin foam rubber sheet in the bottom of the crispers. This stops food getting caught in the ridges and slows the rotting process because air circulates around the food. Foam rubber is available from specialist kitchen shops and department stores. Wash it with washing up liquid and water each time you clean the fridge and dry it on the clothes line.

Clean the rubber seal around the fridge door with a tea towel soaked in white vinegar and bicarb. Then wrap the tea towel over a plastic knife and clean inside all the little grooves. If you can slide a piece of cardboard between the fridge and the seal, it's time to get a new seal. You can buy seals at most hardware shops either sized to fit your model or by the metre. Put them on yourself with an appropriate adhesive.

The exterior of fridges, including stainless-steel ones, should be cleaned with bicarb and white vinegar. Cockroaches are attracted to the warm motor in the fridge so scatter salt underneath to deter them. If you use cockroach baits, put one behind the microwave, one on either side of the bottom of the stove and one behind the fridge.

I recommend cleaning the fridge once a month, but each week you should remove items from the fridge and wipe over the shelves and crispers using either the two-sponge technique or a sponge wrung out in white vinegar with bicarb added. To rinse clean, wipe with a cloth that's been wrung out in water.

For the monthly clean of the fridge, have one storage box and one bin bag with you. Put all the food that's gone off in the bin bag and the other food in the storage box so that you have easy access to the fridge. It's much easier to wipe over a clear shelf than crash and move your jars around as you clean! Using the two-sponge technique, wipe all the shelves, compartments and sides of the fridge. Leave the door open for 2 minutes so the white vinegar can vaporise or it will leave the fridge smelling a bit pickled. Then, if there's any residue, wipe with a cloth wrung out in water. If you like a fragrance, I suggest using vanilla essence. Vanilla has a strong alcohol base, is an antibacterial and the smell won't taint food. Return the items from the storage box to the fridge.

HINT

Many freezers are auto-defrost. Those that aren't need to be defrosted regularly because excess ice transfers flavours from one food source to another. If your ice cream has been tasting a bit fishy lately, it means there's too much ice in the freezer! Even auto-defrost freezers have to be cleaned occasionally. Defrost when ice is greater than 5 mm thick. To do this, remove everything from the fridge and freezer, throw out anything past its use-by date (as marked when the item was first put in the freezer), store other items in an ice-filled cool bag, turn the fridge off and allow the ice to melt. Clean thoroughly before turning the fridge back on and returning the items.

To keep ice at bay, dip a cloth in a solution of 1 table-spoon of white sugar to 240 ml of just-warm water, then wipe the cloth around the freezer. Sugar slows down the production of ice.

Never put a bowl of hot water into a freezer. You could crack the coils and the steam produces more ice crystals. Instead, sprinkle some white sugar over the ice and it will melt more quickly. Sugar doesn't freeze. Never use a hairdryer or heater inside the freezer because it could crack the coils and is very dangerous. Never use a sharp knife or you could pierce the compartment and release the gas, which is also dangerous. Instead, remove the ice with a rubber spatula or with gloved hands.

Storing steel wool

I cleaned an old freezer with fine-grade steel wool and accidentally left the steel wool inside the freezer. When I discovered it,
it didn't have any rust on it. I now store steel wool in a plastic bag
in the freezer to prevent rust.

Problem:	**Odour in the fridge.**
What to use:	**Small divided dish, vanilla essence, bicarb.**
How to apply:	Try to locate the source of the smell and remove it. Then fill a small divided dish with vanilla essence on one side and bicarb on the other. Sushi condiment dishes work well for this. Place the dish in the fridge and it will absorb the nasty smells and deodorise the fridge.

Problem:	**Defrosting the freezer more quickly.**
What to use:	**Sugar, rubber gloves, rubber spatula.**
How to apply:	After turning the fridge off, sprinkle sugar over the base of the freezer. This speeds up the defrosting process. Use gloved hands or a rubber spatula to remove the ice. Never use a hairdryer or heater because it could crack the coils. Never use a sharp knife or you could pierce the coils and release the gas.

Wine coolers with a difference

An unglazed terracotta tile makes a great cooler. Soak one in
water then put it in the freezer ready to use in wine coolers or cool
bags. It also helps the ice last longer. Make your own wine cooler
with a clean unglazed terracotta flowerpot. Soak it in water and
put it in the freezer until you need to use it. The evaporation keeps
the wine chilly. Or create a disposable wine cooler from an old

wine box bladder. Fill the bladder with water and, with the tap on the outside, wrap it around an empty wine bottle. Then put it in the freezer. It's great for picnics because you'll have iced water on tap when it melts as well as chilled wine.

WORKTOPS

Just as you can age a tree by counting its rings, you can age a kitchen by the kind of worktop it has. If it's mission brown, burnt orange or avocado green it's likely to be from the 1970s. Flecked laminate suggests the 1950s. And stainless steel screams 1990s. No matter the fashion, all of them need cleaning and maintenance. If your kitchen is well ventilated but you have persistent smells, it means you have a build-up on your surfaces or in your plumbing. Wipe the worktop thoroughly each time you prepare food.

Laminate

The best way to keep laminate clean is with bicarb and white vinegar applied with sponges. If you get heavy staining with tea or scorch marks, put glycerine on the stain for about 5 minutes then use bicarb and white vinegar. Never use abrasives.

Problem:	**Laminate has come away from chipboard backing or the chipboard is breaking down behind the laminate.**
What to use:	Water, oil of cloves, Unibond PVA, paintbrush, cling film, clamp.
How to apply:	Into 60 ml of warm water, mix 1 drop of oil of cloves and stir thoroughly. Then mix 1 tablespoon of this mixture into 1 tablespoon of Unibond PVA. Paint this over the chipboard, then wrap the entire join in cling

film and clamp it, making sure you have something between the clamp and the bench, such as a magazine or small piece of wood. The mixture will seal the chipboard and the oil of cloves prevents mildew. I learned this after living in some pretty revolting rental properties.

Q: 'I'm living in a rental property at the moment that has a very 1970s yellow laminate worktop,' says John. 'And I don't know how, but I managed to put a hot pot on the laminate and it's left a scald mark. I've tried all the usual cleaners and nothing has worked. How can I fix it so I get my deposit back?'

Problem:	Scald mark on laminate.
What to use:	Cloth, cotton wool ball, Gumption/replacement laminate.
How to apply:	What to do will depend on how deep the burn is. Either way, warm the laminate first with a cloth that's been run under hot water, then wrung out and placed over the affected area. If the scald is deep, put Gumption onto a cotton wool ball and apply the mixture to the scald. Then rinse it off with a damp cloth. If the burn is really bad, you may have to replace a section of the laminate and you'll need a restorer or other professional to help with this.

Q: 'I was on a health kick and decided to make beetroot soup,' says Lisa. 'But the lid flew off the blender and beetroot landed all over the laminate worktop. What can I do?'

Problem: **Beetroot stains on laminate.**

What to use: **White vinegar; or glycerine, cotton bud or cotton wool ball.**

How to apply: If you are dealing with the stain while it's fresh, clean the area with white vinegar. If the stain has set, apply glycerine to the stain with a cotton bud or cotton wool ball; leave for a few minutes then remove with white vinegar. To prevent the problem, put a tea towel over the blender before putting the lid on. If the lid comes off, the tea towel will contain the mess. If the fit is poor, hold the lid on with your hand.

> **HINT**
>
> If you spill hot fat on a worktop, mop it up with a paper towel quickly. Hot fat can burn straight through laminate and can also dissolve glues, so speed is important. After clearing as much fat as possible, wipe the area with bicarb and white vinegar on a sponge.

Corian

Corian is a composite of many different materials including quartz, marble, granite, mica, feldspar and synthetics such as polycarbonate, epoxies or cement blends. Clean with bicarb and white vinegar. If it has a polyurethane finish, use washing up liquid and water.

Clean by sprinkling bicarb then spraying white vinegar and wiping with a sponge. Use washing up liquid and water for a polyurethane finish.

Marble

Marble is often regarded as the glamour worktop. But care should be taken when cleaning it because it's porous. The best way to clean marble is by sprinkling bicarb over it and then lightly spraying 1 part white vinegar to 5 parts water on top. It's important to dilute the white vinegar because full-strength white vinegar can react with the lime in the marble and create holes or a rough surface. Always rinse thoroughly afterwards with a cloth that's been wrung out in water. If the surface isn't sealed with polyurethane or other sealant, use a good quality, liquid hard wax for marble flooring to make it less porous and less likely to absorb stains. The way to tell if marble is covered in polyurethane is to put your eye level with the marble and shine a light along the surface. If the light shines in one uninterrupted beam, it's sealed with polyurethane. If the beam of light has lines and dots, it's unsealed.

Problem:	**Stain in the marble.**
What to use:	**Plaster of Paris, water, washing up liquid.**
How to apply:	If your marble is stained with grease or oil make a paste of plaster of Paris mixed with water to the consistency of peanut butter. For every cup of mixture add 1 teaspoon of washing up liquid. Paint the mixture over the stain to a depth of about 1 cm and leave it to dry completely. Then simply brush the mixture away. It's a good idea to seal the marble when you've cleaned it with a good quality marble flooring wax. If you have trouble finding the flooring wax you can use milk.
Problem:	**White, chalky-looking chips in the marble.**
What to use:	**Candle wax, hairdryer, soft cloth, marble floor wax.**
How to apply:	Match the candle colour to the marble. Place a small piece of wax over the chip, then use a hairdryer to slightly melt the wax into the marble. Buff it with a soft cloth until it's the same height as the rest of the worktop. Then use a marble floor wax to treat the whole area.

Stainless steel

The best way to clean stainless steel is with bicarb and white vinegar. Dust with bicarb, then spray a little white vinegar and wipe with a sponge. Rinse with water and wipe with a cloth to remove any smears. Repeat if necessary.

Problem:	**Scratches in stainless steel.**
What to use:	**Gumption, sponge, bicarb, white vinegar, cloth.**
How to apply:	Apply a dab of Gumption to a sponge and rub it over the scratch. This will smooth the surface. Then sprinkle bicarb over the scratch and spray on a little white vinegar. Remove with a cloth.

Wood

If the wood is unsealed, clean it with washing up liquid and black tea then dry. Then wipe it with good quality furniture oil. For surfaces that come into contact with food, use a small quantity of warm olive oil. Some olive oils contain vegetable sediment, which can attract fruit flies, so make sure you spread it thinly and wipe off all the excess. Only use olive oil on surfaces in the kitchen. Bicarb and white vinegar will remove any stains but remember to reapply the olive oil. If you prefer, keep the timber moist and splinter-free by rubbing it with the peel of a lemon.

For sealed wood, clean with bicarb and white vinegar. Be very careful with polyurethane surfaces because if you scratch them you'll probably have to reseal them. Wipe it with glycerine. If the scratch has penetrated through to the wood, you'll have to reseal the area, which is a big job. If this is the case, seek the advice of a professional.

Problem: Dents in wood.

What to use: Hot wet sponge, hairdryer.

How to apply: Cut a sponge to the size of the dent, wet it in hot water and place it over the dented area only. Leave the sponge for five minutes, take it off and dry the spot with a hairdryer. The wood should have swelled back into place. Don't put hot sponges on any other part of the wood or it will expand it as well.

Problem: Gap between wooden worktop and splashback.

What to use: Disposable rubber gloves, water, matches, candle wax.

How to apply: Put on disposable rubber gloves, wet the tip of your finger with water, then light a candle and feed the dripping wax in between the worktop and splashback with your finger. Candle wax will need to be replaced every six months but it has the added bonus of being easy to replace if needed.

Q: 'I left a melon on a timber worktop and it went off,' says Steve. 'It's left a green stain on the worktop and eaten through the varnish!'

Problem: Rotten melon on wooden worktop.

What to use: Bicarb, white vinegar, nylon brush, varnish.

How to apply: Clean the excess oxide by sprinkling bicarb over the area, add white vinegar and scrub with a nylon brush. Then rinse with water. Allow it to dry and then re-varnish.

Tiles

Tiled worktops need particular care because bacteria can thrive in the grout. Clean tiles and grout by sprinkling bicarb over the surface then spraying white vinegar over the top. Wipe with a cloth then rinse. I'd recommend cleaning tiles more often than other surfaces because grout is so absorbent. Use an old toothbrush to get into tricky areas.

Q: 'We call our 8-year-old son, "Mr Disaster",' confides Ken. 'Recently, he decided to clean our laminex worktop with a scourer and has managed to take all the gloss off. The colour is fine, it's just affected the sheen which is now a bit hazy.'

Problem: Gloss off the worktop.

What to use: Bicarb, white vinegar, nylon brush, cloth, Ceramicoat.

How to apply: There's a spray called Ceramicoat. It's very fast drying so do a test patch first so you become familiar with how it works. Prepare the surface first by sprinkling some bicarb over the area, then sprinkle some white vinegar and rub with a nylon brush. Then rinse with a cloth that's been wrung out in water. Make sure the surface is completely dry, then apply the Ceramicoat in thin, even layers. Ceramicoat is available at ceramics shops.

Chopping boards

A clean chopping board is a hygienic chopping board! They can be made of wood, plastic or glass and I reckon the bigger the better.

Wood should be scrubbed thoroughly after each use with washing up liquid and water and stood up to dry. To prevent splintering, scrub with olive oil and steel wool once a week. Wood has the added benefit of containing a natural antibacterial. Plastic should be cleaned with washing up liquid and water. As soon as it's scuffed, throw it out because scratches harbour bacteria. Clean glass with bicarb and white vinegar.

To make cleaning around the chopping board easier, put a tea towel underneath it to collect crumbs and food spills. It also makes chopping quieter and there's less chance you'll mark the worktop.

SINK

Most kitchen sinks are made of stainless steel or enamel, although some are now made of polycarbonate or cement. The best cleaning combination is bicarb and white vinegar. Clean the sink and buff it. Gumption on a sponge is good for this, but be aware that it contains a mild bleaching agent and abrasive. Don't use abrasives on polycarbonate and always put the cold tap on before the hot tap or it will craze.

Be mindful what you put down the sink. Not only can it be bad for the environment, but you'll also end up creating more work when the sink becomes clogged. Don't put oil, fats, eggs, proteins or starch-based products down it. For fats and oils, re-use an old tin, put a paper towel on the bottom to stop splatter, and collect the waste. When it's full, throw it in the bin.

If you have mildew or bugs under your sink, place some whole cloves and salt inside the cupboard. You could also rub some oil of cloves around the cupboard door edges under the sink. Apply with a cloth.

Problem: **Scratches in stainless-steel sink.**
What to use: **Gumption, sponge, bicarb, white vinegar, cloth.**
How to apply: Apply a dab of Gumption to a sponge and rub it over the scratch. This will smooth the surface. Then sprinkle bicarb over the scratch and splash it with a little white vinegar. Polish with a cloth.

Problem: **Tarnished brass sink ring.**
What to use: **Bicarb, white vinegar, sponge or brush/toothpaste, old toothbrush.**
How to apply: If the sink is discoloured, apply bicarb and white vinegar with a sponge or brush and scrub while it is fizzing. If the ring is badly corroded, put a dab of toothpaste on an old toothbrush and scrub it over the sink ring as though you're cleaning your teeth. Rinse with water.

Problem: **Leaking pipes under the sink.**
What to use: **Hemp rope.**
How to apply: Untwist some hemp rope so that you have about six threads or fibres. Then undo the nut and wind the hemp fibres around the thread on the pipe to seal it. Screw the nut back on over the hemp fibres. The fibres expand as soon as they become wet and this creates a really good seal. This was the technique used before plumber's tape was invented. Hemp rope is also good for leaks at the bottom of the tap and sink.

Problem:	**Smells in the sink drain.**
What to use:	**Bicarb, white vinegar.**
How to apply:	Put 1 tablespoon of bicarb down the drain, followed 20 minutes later by 120 ml of white vinegar. Leave for half an hour. If it's still smelly, do it again. If you have copper or brass pipes, it will smell worse for about half an hour before it gets better. Once it's rinsed through the smell will dissipate.

Problem:	**Black mould in the silicone behind the sink.**
What to use:	**Oil of cloves, bicarb, white vinegar, old tooth-brush/silicone remover, sharp knife, silicone or candle wax.**
How to apply:	First lightly spray with a mixture of 1 teaspoon of oil of cloves in 1 litre of water and leave to dry for a day. To remove the mould detritus sprinkle bicarb over the mould and then spray with white vinegar. Scrub with an old toothbrush then rinse off with water. If this doesn't work, you may need to remove the silicone with a special silicone remover or a very sharp knife. Then replace with new silicone or candle wax.

Washing up by hand

The first rule of washing up is to rinse as much food as possible from plates and cutlery. Rather than leaving the tap running, use a small bucket to rinse items. You can also use paper towels to wipe food off. Put a little hot water in your dirty pots to soak them. Then stack everything needing washing on one side of the sink and have your drying rack on the other side of the sink.

The washing water should be hot, but not too hot. Use a small amount of washing up liquid and wear rubber gloves to prevent slippage. The order to wash things up in is:

1. glassware
2. plastics
3. china
4. cutlery
5. serving dishes
6. pots, pans and cooking utensils

If you have a second sink, keep hot water in it and rinse the item after it's been scrubbed. Then stack the item on the drying rack to air dry or be dried with a tea towel. Air drying is more hygienic.

❏ To avoid streaking, glassware is best drained on a tea towel that has been laid out on the worktop.
❏ Don't put good china or good glassware in water hotter than you could leave your hand in.
❏ Never use steel wool on porcelain or china, no matter how dirty it is. It will scratch the surface, making it porous and vulnerable to dirt and bacteria. If there are ingrained marks, clean them with bicarb and white vinegar.
❏ Never use a scourer or abrasives on polycarbonate glasses because they will scratch the surface. Instead, soak them in warm water with a little washing up liquid. For bad staining, apply glycerine first, then wash in washing up liquid.
❏ To clean your washing gloves, turn them inside out, put them on and wash your hands in soap. Then leave them inside out to dry.

HINT

Detergent

Detergent acts as an emulsifier for fats and oils, which means it allows grease to mix with water and helps lift it off surfaces. Oils and fats are what make most types of dirt stick to other objects. When you break them down, you make it easier to clean off the dirt. Detergents are not all antibacterial, though many people assume they are. The other mistake people make is using too much detergent when washing up – more is not better. If you use too much, you'll have to rinse items after washing up because it will leave a soap residue – and bacteria can thrive in soap residue! You simply need to balance the amount of detergent with the amount of grease you're cleaning. With a good-quality liquid, 1 teaspoon of washing up liquid per sink of hot water should be plenty. You can tell by the amount of bubbles in the water. You need only 2 cm of foam on the top of the water for a standard sink of dishes. When the bubbles disappear, it's time for some fresh water and washing up liquid. Once all the washing up has been done and the dish rack is stacked, tip a jug of warm water over the clean dishes to rinse away any detergent. Allow the water to drain, leaving the dishes clean and shiny. Then, if you must, dry them with a clean tea towel.

HINT

Tea towels

I suggest changing tea towels every two days but if you use the tea towel for anything other than drying, such as an oven mitt or for catching crumbs and wiping hands, be on the safe side and put it in the wash every day. After using them, hang tea towels out to dry or bacteria will breed in them. To clean tea towels, wash them in the washing machine or, if they're really soiled, first soak them in Vanish before putting them through the washing machine.

HINT

Kitchen cloths

There is an increasing range of kitchen cloths and sponges available these days. While the newer ones are much better at picking up dirt, they're also more likely to hold bacteria because of the greater surface area. Those hairy bits simply offer more spots for bacteria to live in. My preference is to recycle rags or old tights from the rag bag. There's no need to buy expensive cleaning cloths when an old T-shirt does the job really well. Either rip up the old T-shirt or cut it with scissors to the size you need. An important rule with kitchen cloths is not to contaminate your food preparation area. I suggest using different coloured sponges or cloths according to where they're used.

Replace the nylon washing-up brush when the bristles are bent out of shape, but don't throw away the worn ones. Keep them for other uses, such as to clean outside under ledges and around pot plants in the garden and for scrubbing spot stains on the kitchen floor.

Taps

Taps can be made of stainless steel, chrome, brass or powder coated. Except for powder-coated taps, clean with bicarb and white vinegar. To clean the backs of taps, use an old pair of tights. Wrap the leg around the tap and move it in a sawing motion backwards and forwards. Powder coating is a form of plastic that is heat sealed onto the surface of metal to colour it. Powder-coated taps are often cream, white or black. Don't use any abrasives on them, just wash with soap and water and always turn your cold tap on first or the powder coating will chip and discolour.

DRAINS

Drains are designed to take things away but they can also provide an entry for other things, such as insects. To stop insects gaining entry, put flyscreen material behind the drain grill. This will prevent blockages as well. To keep cockroaches away, wipe a solution of salt and water around the drain.

If your drain is blocked, put 60 g of bicarb down, then add 120 ml of white vinegar and leave for half an hour. If your pipes are old and made of iron, using a caustic cleaner is not only bad for the environment, but could pit the surface of the pipe (caustic is an oxidising agent and eats into iron), which also means it will hold bacteria.

CUPBOARDS

The more often you wipe your cupboards, the cleaner they will stay. If you can, give them a quick wipe every day. And don't forget about the surface on top of the cupboard. Many kitchen cupboards now go right up to the ceiling, which removes this task, but if you have exposed cupboards, you'll be amazed at how much dust and grease gathers here. As much as you'd like to adopt the 'out of sight, out of mind' approach, the dust that settles here will gradually spread around the rest of the kitchen. To cut back on cleaning, put paper – even newspaper will do – on top of cupboards and change it each month. It's much easier doing this than scrubbing later on.

The best time to clean the underside of wall-mounted cupboards is after making soup or boiling the kettle because the steam softens the grease and grime.

The easiest way to clean inside your kitchen drawers is to vacuum them every couple of weeks, then wipe with a damp cloth. If you haven't cleaned them in a while, use bicarb and white vinegar, then wipe with a cloth that has been soaked in hot water.

CROCKERY

Most people have plates for everyday use and another set for special occasions. Crockery can be made of china, porcelain, pottery, glass or polycarbonate resin. Those in everyday use can be washed in washing up liquid and water. Never soak pottery as it can lift the glaze. To prevent your good china chipping and cracking in cupboards, put a small piece of paper towel in between the plates. This also helps prevent wear and tear on them. Never put gold-rimmed china in the microwave or dishwasher.

In terms of where plates and dishes should be stored, I apply the principle that anything you eat off should be stored above waist height because of insects. Anything kept below waist level should be washed before being used. Make sure pots and pans are completely dry before putting them away to prevent mould and corrosion.

> **HINT**
>
> Don't store china and metal on top of one another because the metal will leave a 'tile mark', which is like a pencil mark. To remove, use a soft pencil eraser.

Problem:	**Plates with discoloured crazing.**
What to use:	**Effervescing overnight denture soaker.**
How to apply:	Add 2 tablets of denture soaker to a sink full of hot water. Put the plates in the sink and leave overnight. Rinse them off in clean water then leave them in the sun, if possible. Dry them very well. No matter what anyone tells you, do not soak china in bleach. It's bad for the environment and the bleach can lift the glaze and cause a white powdery coating that won't go away.

Problem: Stained teacups/teapots.
What to use: Bicarb, white vinegar, nylon brush.
How to apply: Mix 1 teaspoon of bicarb with 1 tablespoon of white vinegar. Rub it inside the teacup or teapot with a nylon brush. Rinse in clean water.

Problem: Chips in crockery.
What to use: Denture soaker, glycerine/sapphire nail file, glycerine or heat-resistant superglue.
How to apply: This is only a temporary solution. Clean the plate in a sink full of hot water with 2 tablets of denture soaker added to it. Allow the plate to dry thoroughly in sunlight. Then soak the chip with glycerine to seal it. It's best to throw chipped crockery away because bacteria can get into the porous surface. For special pieces, see a professional restorer.

If you have a sharp chip, file with a sapphire nail file (a file that contains ground sapphire and will grind glass) around the edge of the chip, not down or across the chip. Then treat with glycerine. You can also use heat-resistant superglue to seal the chip.

If you have grey lines across a plate, it means the seal has gone and dirt has penetrated into the plate. Rather than throw it away, add it to your recycle box to use as a pot plant saucer or something else. See a restorer for valuable pieces.

Salt and pepper

To keep the salt in your shaker loose, add rice to it. To keep pepper loose, use dried peas. Adding dried peas also keeps parmesan cheese loose.

CUTLERY

Wash cutlery in washing up liquid and water. If it's very dirty, stained or has rust spots, use bicarb and white vinegar first. Gold cutlery should only be cleaned with bicarb and white vinegar.

Brass, copper, silver and pewter cutlery can also be cleaned in an old aluminium saucepan with 60 g of bicarb dissolved in 900 ml of hot water. Put the cutlery in and leave it for a few minutes. **Don't put your bare hands into the water because they will burn.** Wear rubber gloves or use wooden kitchen tools or skewers to manipulate the pieces. Then rinse the cutlery with water and white vinegar. Never add water to the aluminium pot after cleaning – pour the solution out first – as it can boil over because of the reaction between the aluminium, baking soda and hot water.

An old-fashioned way to get a glass-like polish on silverware is to rub it with a paste of unprocessed wheat bran and white vinegar. Put cotton gloves or a pair of old cotton socks on your hands to stop the acid from your hands affecting the silver. Clean the paste off, then polish with a cloth. Remove scratches from silverware by rubbing a handful of unprocessed wheat bran over it with your hand. Don't use proprietary sprays that contain silicone. Clean pewter with wheat bran and white vinegar but be careful not to overpolish it or you'll remove the patina of age and devalue the piece.

To clean, polish and seal bone handles on cutlery, mix 20 parts sweet almond oil to 1 part oil of cloves and mix thoroughly. Then rub this mixture over the handles. If the handles have become dry and cracked, leave them soaking in the mixture. After soaking, polish with a clean cloth. If the bone is very dirty, clean it first with bicarb and a little water. Never use heat with bone because it will discolour and crack.

Q: 'I'd like to know how to stop the dishwasher leaving rust on my stainless-steel cutlery,' says Nicole.

Problem: **Rust on cutlery.**
What to use: **Bicarb, white vinegar.**
How to apply: The dishwasher sandblasts your cutlery and creates rust marks. Polish the cutlery by hand with a paste of white vinegar and bicarb, wipe, then rinse off in water.

Q: 'I've got green marks on my Thai copper cutlery,' says Susan. 'Do they come off?'

Problem: **Green marks on copper cutlery.**
What to use: **Bicarb, white vinegar, nylon brush.**
How to apply: Lay the cutlery in the sink and sprinkle bicarb over it, then splash white vinegar on top. Scrub with a nylon brush and rinse. The reason Thais use copper cutlery is because curries taste sweeter when eaten with copper. Silver gives curries an acidic tang.

HINT

If you boil new wooden utensils for 10 minutes in a saucepan with enough cider white vinegar to cover them, it seals the wood and protects against smells and splintering. This is particularly good for wooden spoons used for making curries. To remove a curry stain, soak the wooden spoon in glycerine for a couple of days, then wash.

Also sweeten the smell of a room where curry has been cooked, by slicing a lemon, placing it on a saucer and pressing down on the lemon to release its juices. It gives the room a fresh rather than a stale smell.

KITCHEN KNIVES

When I was young, I remember seeing a Chinese chef creating sculptures out of vegetables with his Chinese chopper. It was a fantastic sight to witness. I later learned that half the skill lies in having a good knife! Choose the best you can afford. I suggest using a Chinese chopper, a large carving knife, a carving knife with a curved blade, a serrated bread knife, a serrated vegetable knife and a paring knife. Choose high-quality steel and ensure handles are solid and well secured.

If you use the wrong tools to sharpen knives, they'll rust. Only sharpen them with a steel and a whetstone. Never use cheap wheel sharpeners or you'll demagnetise the blades and get rust spots. And never use steel wool to clean a knife because it'll rust. If in doubt, use a professional knife sharpener. I suggest asking your local restaurant when their knife sharpener is coming and arranging to have yours sharpened at the same time.

If you keep recipe books in the kitchen, wipe them each week and spray them with a non-toxic insecticide spray as they attract insects.

GLASSWARE

The worst things for glass are extreme heat, extreme cold, chemicals and abrasives. To protect your good glassware, avoid putting it in the dishwasher. As I've said before, I hate dishwashers, particularly when it comes to glass, because it becomes scratched and cloudy-looking and this damage is permanent. Don't soak glassware in washing up liquid or use strong bleach products. Just use water.

To prevent crystal becoming cloudy, only wash it in water no hotter than you can leave your hands in. Add a small amount of white vinegar to the wash to prevent spotting and fogging.

To clean dirt out of champagne glasses or glassware that has narrow apertures, put a little olive oil in the glass first and leave for a few minutes. The oil collects and lifts the dust. Then get a thin, long-handled paintbrush, wrap sticky tape around the ferrule, or silver part, and rub it around the difficult-to-reach area. Wash the glasses in washing up liquid and water. If it's too narrow for a thin paintbrush, use a bamboo skewer and chew the end of it until it's shaped like a brush.

- ❏ Always put a tea towel in the bottom of the sink in case you drop a piece while your hands are wet. The tea towel will cushion the impact.
- ❏ Never leave wine sitting in glasses because it will leave a mark.
- ❏ To remove lipstick on the edge of glasses, dip a small cotton wool ball in white vinegar and wipe over the lipstick.
- ❏ Never twist a tea towel through a stemmed glass as the glass could snap.

HINT

Glasses, plates and dishes: should you store glasses facing up or down?

This is a guaranteed conversation starter and a bit like the debate over which way the toilet paper should hang. This is what I do and why I do it. Glasses stored on shelves above eye level should face upwards to remind you to rinse them out before using them. This is because you can't see if the shelves are dusty. Glasses stored on shelves below eye level should face downwards. This is because you can see if the cupboard shelf is dirty and if the glass needs to be rinsed before using it.

Problem: Soap scum on glass.
What to use: White vinegar, water, cloth.
How to apply: Mix 1 tablespoon of white vinegar with 240 ml of water. Place the glass in the mixture. Then polish dry with a cloth.

Q:

Gabrielle puts everything in the dishwasher. 'But I've noticed I'm getting white marks on my glasses. What can I do about this?'

Problem: Whiteness on glass.
What to use: Sweet almond oil.
How to apply: If it's soap scum, see above. If it's been scratched, the damage is permanent. You may be able to alleviate the problem with sweet almond oil soaked in a cloth; however, this only works on some pieces and you don't know which ones will respond until you do it.

Problem: Tiny chips on the edge of your glass.
What to use: Sapphire nail file.
How to apply: Place the nail file horizontally and flat to the rim of the glass and slowly buff along the chips. Never go across or down the glass.

DID YOU KNOW? If you drop a glass on the ground, make sure you've collected all the shards by lying a lit torch on the floor so the beam goes across the floor. Any remaining shards will sparkle in the light. Make sure you wear shoes and gloves when clearing glass.

How to remove sticky labels

I come from a family that always removed labels from jars before putting them on the table because it was considered the polite thing to do. And, because it was the era before plastic containers, we used glass jars for everything! There are several ways to remove sticky labels from glass and plastic containers. One method is to fill them with hot water, close the lid tightly and leave for a few minutes. Then lift the edge of the sticker slowly with a blunt knife. If any adhesive remains, wipe it with tea tree oil. Another way is to lay down a piece of cling film just bigger than the sticker. Mix one drop of washing up liquid with a small quantity of water in a spray pack, spray it over the cling film then place the cling film over the sticker. Leave for five minutes, or longer if the glue is very strong. The sticker will come off with the cling film. Don't try to remove the label by placing the jar itself into hot water – even though the paper will dissolve, the glue won't and you'll be left with a sticky mess that you'll have to rub and rub and rub.

CHAIRS AND STOOLS

If you have chairs or stools in the kitchen, wipe them with a cloth that's been wrung out in water because they are great dust collectors. And don't forget to clean the legs as well.

HINT

If you drop an egg on the floor, don't use a sponge to clean it up or you'll spread the mess. If you have a pair of squeegees, push them together and lift the egg into a bowl. If you don't have squeegees, get two pieces of thick cardboard, place them either side of the egg spill, and move them towards each other, collecting the egg as you go.

Place the egg in a bowl then throw it in the bin. When most of the egg has been removed, use a paper towel dampened with washing up liquid to eradicate all traces of the mess. Always use cold water as cooked egg is harder to remove.

TABLES AND WORKTOPS

No matter how busy or tired you are, you must wipe tables and worktops daily. If you don't, your food preparation zone will become a paradise for nasties such as cockroaches. If you're wavering, just picture yourself coming to the kitchen in the middle of the night to see something scary scurrying across the worktop. It's the last thing you need.

Make sure you wipe the whole work surface and don't forget the area underneath the toaster and kettle. These appliances may hide crumbs to your eyes, but cockroaches will sniff them out a street away.

> **HINT**
>
> Children love things that fizz. Have them help you clean the worktops by sprinkling over some bicarb, then adding white vinegar. They'll love the reaction the two make when they come into contact – the fizzing also tickles their fingers!

Recycling and containers

Many people have lost the art of recycling. So much stuff just gets thrown into the bin. It's very easy to get into the habit of reusing materials and one of the best ways is to create a space for recycled items. I keep an area near my back door for items that can be recycled and reused. The garage is another good spot. Just make sure the area is under cover and protected from the weather.

One of the easiest things to recycle is glass jars. Just clean them when you do the daily washing up and store them in your recycling area. Remember: if you're going to use them to store food, you need to sterilise them. Heating the jars in a hot oven is the best way to do this.

Reuse old tins: you could store old cooking fat in them, they are handy containers for nuts and bolts and you could even use them to soak paint brushes in.

Egg cartons are great for germinating seeds. They're even better for holding children's paints. See if your local primary school or craft centre would like your old ones. If you buy your eggs at a farm shop, you could also take them back and reuse the carton – many are pleased to do this. Plastic squeeze-top bottles make great paint containers for kids. Keep bits of old string, tie them together and roll them into a ball. That way you'll have string ready to use whenever you need it. Keep elastic bands in a container to use again. Cereal cartons can be recycled into filing trays. Decorate them to become storage for children's toys.

Keep plastic bags and store them in a plastic bag holder. This is a fabric tube with elastic at either end and a loop to hang it from. You stuff new bags in the top and pull out old bags from the bottom. Plastic bags can be washed over and over.

Plastic takeaway food containers can be used for so many things. They're particularly great for keeping leftovers in, then doubling as a lunch box. Wash them and reuse them. To get rid of the greasy feel, put a little white vinegar in the water when you're rinsing.

You could even recycle old leather shoes to become pot plant holders!

Sweet-smelling hands

Rubbing your hands with bicarb and white vinegar removes smells, especially after working with onions, garlic or chilli. An alternative is to wear disposable gloves when chopping.

THE PANTRY OR LARDER

If you organise your pantry by keeping similar items together, you won't waste time searching for things. If you don't have enough room in your pantry, think about putting another shelf in. Or get some free-standing wire shelves that are stackable.

Keep grain foods separately because insects such as moths, cockroaches and weevils are attracted to them. Once you open any packet, put the contents in an air-tight container and mark the contents and use-by date on it. I like to cut the relevant information from the packet and sticky tape or glue it to the jar. You can also seal a packet with an old bread clip or bulldog clip. If you do get moths, use bay leaves or bay oil. Two bay leaves per shelf should do the job, add a couple of drops of bay oil to a cloth and wipe over the shelves. If you have a serious insect problem, wipe the shelves once a month. If you don't have a serious insect problem, wipe the shelves once every three months. Another way to prevent weevils in grain food is to make a small cling film bag, fill it full of salt, seal the top and prick the bag with pinholes. Place this inside the containers. I always remove cereals from the cardboard box because insects are attracted to cardboard. Seal the plastic liner with a peg or old bread clip.

Most canned food will last from two to four years, but the earlier you consume it, the better. Most cans have a use-by date on them. If they don't, write the date of purchase on the side. I learned the hard way when a can exploded in the pantry. It's an experience I don't want to repeat any time soon!

Refrigerate jars such as mayonnaise and mustard after opening. Oils will go off and become rancid. You should only store them for about six months. Rather than buying expensive oil sprays, put oil in your own spray pack. Oils react differently when heated and some leave more grease than others on your kitchen cupboards.

Rapeseed oil is the worst for leaving oily scum as it seems to fume more. I bought a cheap drum of it once thinking it was a bargain but it was costly in cleaning-up terms! As a rule, the better the quality of the oil, the less splattering you're likely to get. Have a range of oils available so you use the right oil for the job. For example, don't use olive oil for chips because the oil will burn before the chips are cooked.

Place a layer of paper towel in the bottom of a sugar container to prevent lumping and clumping. If you put a piece of terracotta in your brown sugar it won't clot.

Always keep your dried herbs tightly sealed in glass or plastic and out of strong sunlight. Buy them in small quantities because they lose their flavour after about six months. Even better, grow them fresh on your windowsill.

Wipe along the pantry shelves, but don't worry about extensive cleaning until the spring clean. The easiest way to clean inside your kitchen drawers is to vacuum them every couple of weeks, then wipe with a cloth wrung out in water. If you haven't cleaned them in a while, use bicarb and white vinegar, then wipe with a cloth that has been soaked in hot water. If you have unsealed wooden kitchen drawers, clean with a cloth that's been tightly wrung out in hot water then dry the area before returning the utensils. These drawers should be sealed with contact paper or a liner of some form because raw timber attracts insects and isn't hygienic for cutlery.

 'We've got these pesky moths in the pantry that seem to breed in anything and everything,' says Michael. 'Can we get rid of them?'

Problem:	**Moths in the pantry.**
What to use:	**Bay leaves, bay oil or mint tea, cloth.**
How to apply:	Place 1 dried bay leaf every 30 cm along the shelves or apply bay oil to a cloth and then wipe over the shelves or wipe the shelves with a very strong mint tea. Reapply regularly.

COMMON KITCHEN PESTS

Cockroaches

The cockroach is high on most people's list of most-hated pests. And they are really difficult to get rid of. Here is a non-chemical strategy. This option uses salt. I use swimming pool salt because it's much cheaper, but table salt works just as well. Using a salt shaker, scatter salt along the edge of the skirting board in the kitchen, including under the fridge. Salt is absorbed through the underside carapace of the cockroach which dehydrates and kills them. One reason they're so hard to kill is that, before they die, they drop their egg case, which, in German cockroaches, contains about 40 eggs that hatch in 28–30 days. If the egg case falls on the salt, the nymphs that hatch out dehydrate and die. It is also a good idea to rinse around drains with a salt solution and use flyscreen netting underneath floor wastes and drain holes. Cockroaches don't like salt and the netting stops larger ones from getting inside. The netting keeps spiders out as well. Cockroaches love moist, fatty, meaty, sweet, dark environments with lots of organic material. They stay away from light, dry and salty environments. I once had a house with a serious cockroach problem, so I removed all the doors on the kitchen cupboards to let in as much light as possible. Insects prefer dark to light, so this helped keep them at bay and allowed me to keep an eye on them.

Mice

Dried snake poo placed in the corners or rooms (out of reach of little fingers) can be used to keep mice at bay. Get some from a zoo or try your local pet shops. Access points can be blocked with a wad of steel wool. You could also use a mousetrap, but rather than cheese, use a fresh pumpkin seed as bait. Mice love pumpkin seeds.

Ants

You will probably only be able to see part of the ant trail and you need to find the rest of it so you can locate the nest. Put some talcum powder on the trail and the ants will carry it and mark the rest of the trail. Then find the ant nest and pour boiling water into it.

Flies

Wipe lavender oil on door frames and window frames. You could also put 1 teaspoon of lavender oil on a small piece of sponge, add 2 tablespoons of hot water and leave this in a saucer. Top up the solution each week. Or try filling a spray bottle with lavender oil and spray trouble spots regularly.

And here's an old-fashioned fly poison from *Lee's Priceless Recipes*, 1817: with ½ ounce of sugar and ½ ounce of finely ground black pepper, mix with a small amount of water to create a thin paste. Place it on a piece of paper where flies congregate. They eat it and die!

Mosquitoes

Keep lavender oil in a spray bottle of water and spray when needed.

CHAPTER 4:
The Bathroom

Bathrooms seem to be multiplying as fast as rabbits. The absolute minimum now appears to be two; master bedrooms must have an ensuite and larger homes have as many bathrooms as bedrooms. And let's not forget the toilet and shower downstairs! We want all of these to be immaculate. And not just for us; no one wants guests discovering a mouldy ceiling, dirty tiles or something worse in one of our many ablution centres. The bathroom is one of the easiest rooms in the house to look after because it's designed to be cleaned – and when you've finished, the room sparkles from floor to ceiling. Remember: always work from top to bottom. As you know, I love to clean with bicarb and white vinegar but you may prefer to use proprietary products. Whatever you use, make sure you rinse any product thoroughly. Never use steel wool on any surface in the bathroom or you'll create scratch marks.

ASSEMBLE THE CLEAN KIT

bicarb – cleaning agent
bucket – to hold water or to hold cleaning items
cloth (such as an old T-shirt) – to wipe surfaces and absorb water
clutter bucket – to transport displaced items
denture cleaner – to remove marks in the bath
detergent (washing up liquid) – cleaning agent
dustpan and brush – to clear accumulated dirt
glycerine – to prime surfaces
Gumption – cleaning agent
lavender oil – cleaner and fragrance
mop – to wipe over floors
nylon broom – to sweep floors and clear cobwebs
nylon scrubbing brush – to aid cleaning
oil of cloves – to deter mould

old stockings – to clean soap scum
old toothbrush – to access tight corners
old towel – to absorb water
paper towel – to absorb water
rubber gloves – to protect hands and provide grip
sponge or rags – to use as cleaning cloths
spray bottle – to spray white vinegar
vacuum cleaner – to vacuum floors
water – cleaning and rinsing
white vinegar – cleaning agent

CLEANING SPECIFIC TO THE BATHROOM

Remove anything that doesn't belong in the bathroom into your
clutter bucket. Then remove any loose items, such as towels, toilet
paper, toothbrushes and bin, and store them outside the bathroom.
Put all the plugs in the sink holes, including the bath, and cover the
shower drain hole. Run the water from all the taps on hot until the
room is really steamy and therefore easier to clean. Watch that you
don't create a flood of water – and make sure you don't put the
extractor fan on! Then remove the plugs. Alternatively you may
want to save water by cleaning straight after you or someone else
in the house has had a shower.

Sprinkle bicarb over the bath, sink, shower and toilet. With white
vinegar in a spray bottle, squirt the bicarb and scrub either with a
sponge, scrubbing brush or a pair of old stockings rolled up into a
ball. Stockings cut through soap scum really well. Clean behind taps
by wrapping a stocking around the base of the taps and sawing
backwards and forwards. Don't forget the areas around the drains.
Clean the toilet. Wipe the walls using the two-sponge technique or
use one sponge dipped in bicarb and a spray bottle of white vinegar.

Clean a tiled floor by sprinkling over bicarb then spraying with white vinegar. As they're fizzing, rub over with a nylon brush or nylon broom. Rinse with water. Use a broom to access the ceiling and give it a good sweep. Once you've scrubbed every surface, including the towel rail, rinse with water or you can use a spray bottle filled with water. Just be very careful around electrical fittings. For really stubborn stains on your sink, bath, toilet or any tiled surface, use Gumption on a cloth.

If your grout is mouldy, wipe with bicarb and white vinegar and scrub with an old toothbrush. To inhibit mould, add a couple of drops of oil of cloves to the mixture.

If you have unsealed wood, vinyl wallpaper or other surfaces that shouldn't be left wet, dry them with either old cloth nappies or old towels from the rag bag. Tie the towelling to your broom head with elastic bands and wipe the walls.

Finish by drying surfaces, including the bath, with an old towel. This prevents water marks and leaves a sparkling finish. To clean the inside of bathroom windows, use a squeegee and water. If the window is grimy, use 240 ml of white vinegar to a bucket of warm water.

The bathroom is an easy place for clutter to gather. I suggest having a stash of plastic tie bags so you can regularly remove clutter. If your cupboard space is under the sink, be careful what you store here because it can be a moisture trap. It's better to store items high and dry. Buy small storage units, preferably without doors, to organise all that bathroom paraphernalia, such as hair gel, cotton buds and dental floss.

 Q: 'I've got a beautiful old marble vanity top,' says Deborah. 'But the look of it is marred by some circles of rust that I can't remove. It's such a pity because the marble is so beautiful. Is there any way of removing them?'

Problem: **Rust on marble.**
What to use: **Plaster of Paris, water, washing up liquid, salt.**
How to apply: If your marble is stained with rust make a paste of
plaster of Paris mixed with water to the consistency
of peanut butter. For every cup of mixture add half a
teaspoon of salt and and paint the mixture over the
stain to a depth of about 1 cm. Leave it to dry
completely and then simply brush the mixture away.
The rust stains were probably caused by the bottom
of a hairspray can. Most cans are unsealed, and
when they interact with water they rust. One way to
prevent this is to paint clear nail polish on the
bottom of any cans that sit on the vanity top.

Q: 'I've got these little black flying insects in my
bathroom,' reports Sam. 'They gravitate towards the
roof. Is there anything I can do?'

Problem: **Black bugs in bathroom.**
What to use: **Salt, water, sponge.**
How to apply: These could be a variety of fruit flies. Many
shampoos have fruit oil in them, which attracts
some bugs. Make sure your shampoo is sealed and
keep the tops of the containers clean. If the insects
are beetles, make a solution of salt and water and
paint it around your drains and windowsills with a
sponge.

TOILET

Has anyone shown you how to clean the toilet properly? I'll assume
'no' was the answer to that question. This is my approach using

bicarb and white vinegar. I don't like using toilet mats and toilet seat covers because they harbour bacteria, smells and they create more cleaning. But if you do have them, make sure you wash them once a week.

Always have a bin near the toilet. That way there's no excuse for people leaving empty toilet rolls lying around near the toilet!

Tools:	Bicarb, sponges, white vinegar, toilet brush.
Technique:	1. Flush the toilet to wet the sides of the bowl.
	2. Sprinkle bicarb over the inside of the bowl.
	3. Wipe the top of the cistern using the two-sponge technique with bicarb and white vinegar.
	4. Wipe the top of the lid, under the lid, the top of the seat and under the seat using the same technique.
	5. Splash white vinegar over the bicarb in the bowl, then use a toilet brush to scrub, including up and around the rim.
	6. Wipe the top of the rim with a sponge.
	7. Wash the sponge in hot water and wipe again.
	8. Flush.
	9. Rinse the sponge and wipe the outside of the toilet bowl right to the floor, including the plumbing at the back.
	10. Congratulations, you're done!

The ping-pong ball technique

If you have a young boy who's having difficulty getting all his pee in the bowl, put a ping-pong ball at the bottom of the toilet and tell him to aim for it. The ping-pong ball won't flush because it's too light and you'll be surprised at how much better his aim becomes.

Problem: Bad stains on the inside of the toilet bowl.

What to use: Small plastic cup, bicarb, white vinegar, nylon brush.

How to apply: Turn the tap off at the cistern. Drain the bottom of the bowl with a small plastic cup. Then sprinkle bicarb over the bowl and splash some white vinegar over the bicarb. Scrub with a nylon brush. Turn the water back on at the cistern.

Q: 'We've got orange rust stains on our toilet bowl from bore water,' says Sue. 'How can we remove them?'

Problem: Rust stains/hard-water fur.

What to use: Descaler, rubber gloves, mask.

How to apply: Put half a cap of descaler into the cistern, leave it for an hour, then flush the toilet. This will help prevent the bowl staining as it cleans the fur out of the cistern. For heavy stains, clean the bowl with descaler but make sure you use rubber gloves and a mask. Note that descaler should only be used to remove staining and not as a regular cleaner.

Problem: Dirty seat.

What to use: Bicarb, white vinegar, sponge/Gumption/sweet almond oil or glycerine.

How to apply: For plastic seats, sprinkle bicarb then wipe a white vinegar-soaked sponge over the top. For Bakelite seats, put a dab of Gumption on a sponge and wipe it over the seat. Then rinse with water. If you've lost that glossy look on your Bakelite toilet seat, rub a drop of sweet almond oil on it. If it's plastic, rub it with glycerine.

Problem:	Urine smell.
What to use:	A lemon, ice-cream container, water/white vinegar, water.
How to apply:	Wash surfaces with the juice from half a lemon added to an ice-cream container of water. Alternatively, use white vinegar and water. Lemon is preferable because it leaves a nice smell. It's particularly important to wipe the pipes at the back of the toilet.

Q: 'I've got a nasty black mark on the water line of my toilet,' says John. 'I just can't shift it. What should I do?'

Problem:	Unwanted black line in toilet.
What to use:	Descaler, plastic cup, bicarb, white vinegar, brush.
How to apply:	Place a capful of descaler into the cistern of the toilet. Leave it for 10 minutes then flush. Then leave it again for another 10 minutes. Then turn the tap off at the cistern and drain the water from the bowl with a small plastic cup. Then wipe the mark with bicarb and white vinegar and scrub with a brush. Turn water back on then flush.

Problem:	Rubber beginning to perish.
What to use:	Salt, glycerine, talcum powder, cloth.
How to apply:	Rub the perish marks with salt, wipe over with glycerine and then sprinkle with talcum powder. When dry, remove the talcum powder with a cloth. If the rubber has perished too much, you'll need to replace it.

Using the toilet brush each time you use the toilet will speed up your cleaning. If you scrub it straight away, there will be less cleaning to do later. Leave the toilet brush inside the toilet as you flush and it will clean the brush as well.

DID YOU KNOW? Lavender oil removes light water staining in the toilet. Add 1 drop of lavender oil every three days to create a cleaning film. If the stain is really bad, add 1/2 capful of descaler to the cistern water.

Toilet rolls

In days gone by, Barbie-like dolls called 'dress-a-dolls' became a popular toilet-roll storage solution. They were much loved by grandmothers, but if they only knew how much bacteria lived in the skirts, they'd be horrified! These days, many people keep spare toilet rolls on the cistern but I think you should avoid this because it's too easy for the roll to fall into the toilet. I store toilet rolls on a giant wooden spike with a thick base so water doesn't get onto the bottom of the toilet paper and make it frilly. Pile them as high as you like or use several spikes. I use unscented toilet rolls because many people are sensitive to the chemicals. If you like having a scent, you can create your own. Simply spray a small amount of lavender oil onto the cardboard inside the toilet roll. Cardboard absorbs the lavender smell and continually recirculates it.

HINT

Is it okay to use bleach?
Bleach is a cleaning agent and an antibacterial, but it's also quite corrosive and high in phosphates and bad for the environment. I much prefer to use bicarb and white vinegar. Simply sprinkle on bicarb then sprinkle on white vinegar and, when it's fizzing, scrub with a nylon brush or broom, then rinse.

Non-toxic air freshener
I suffer from asthma and proprietary sprays make me wheeze so I created this non-toxic bathroom air freshener. Fill a spray pack with water and add 2 drops of washing up liquid and 5 drops of lavender oil. You can substitute other essential oils except those with high colouring levels, such as stone fruits. Eucalyptus oil should be used sparingly because it will mark painted surfaces. Spray as needed.

BATH

Taking a bath is one of life's great luxuries. Most baths are made of vitreous china, although new ones are made of acrylic, fibreglass or polycarbonate. You may also encounter stainless-steel, metal or cast-iron baths. Use bicarb and white vinegar to clean them or, if they're very dirty, Gumption. An old pair of stockings rolled into a ball is great to clean with because it cuts through soap scum really well without scratching. Never use steel wool to clean baths or you'll leave scratch marks.

If you have a cast-iron bath, don't put hot water in first. Cast iron shrinks and expands at a different rate to the enamel covering and, if the water is too hot, you'll get chips and cracks. Put a little cold water in cast-iron and polycarbonate baths first.

When cleaning the bath, clean the tiles above the bath first, then the taps, then the sides and bottom of the bath. Then rinse. Never use abrasives on polycarbonate baths. Use glycerine to remove stains. Keep a rolled up pair of tights near the bath and have users wipe the bath down after having one, or the handbasin after shaving. It'll help prevent those unattractive dirt rings.

Problem:	**Rust stains on the sink ring.**
What to use:	**Rubber gloves, descaler, cloth.**
How to apply:	Put on rubber gloves then wipe descaler on the sink ring with a cloth. Wipe it off then rinse.

Problem:	**Scratches in fibreglass.**
What to use:	**Glycerine, 2000-grade wet-and-dry.**
How to apply:	Put glycerine on the wet-and-dry and rub over the scratch.

> **HINT**
>
> If there are drip marks in the bath or sink use a little descaler applied with a cotton wool ball, cotton bud or nylon brush.

Spa baths

At the press of a button, a bath is transformed into a bubbling comfort zone. Clean spa baths the same way as regular baths, but look out for chalk deposits, body fat and skin cell build-up. Chalk deposits come about because soap and water is flushed backwards and forwards at different temperatures. Remove with white vinegar and clean the nozzle regularly with descaler. After every couple of uses, run white vinegar and water through the spa.

HINT

If your bath has gone yellow
Bleach can often make modern bath surfaces turn yellow.
Fill the bath with warm water and add 1 packet of denture
tablets or powder. Leave overnight and drain the water.

HINT

If your bath has grey marks
It could mean bleach has taken off the porcelain coating
and left an absorbent surface where dirt has lodged. To
alleviate the problem, fill the bath with water and add 1
packet of denture cleaner. The denture cleaner can be in
tablet or powder form. Leave overnight. Then wipe the
surface with glycerine to seal it. If you use the bath often,
you'll need to wipe the surface with glycerine every three
months. The grey marks could also be created by
contact with metallic objects such as steel wool or back
scratchers made with stainless steel. Clean these marks
by sprinkling on bicarb, adding white vinegar and
scrubbing with a nylon brush or rub with a pencil eraser.

Q: 'We live in the Australian bush,' says Joanne. 'And
use dam water which has really stained the bath. Is
there any way of repairing it?

Problem: **Dirty-looking bath.**
What to use: **Descaler, cloth.**
How to apply: Use a descaler and follow the instructions on the
packet with one variation. Dilute the mixture to half
the recommended strength. Then wipe it over the
surface of the bath with a cloth. Then rinse with
water.

> **HINT**
>
> Create your own air freshener by filling a spray bottle with water, add 2 drops of washing up liquid and 5 drops of lavender oil. Leave it near the toilet. You can also use tea tree oil or any of the floral essential oils.

SHOWER

It might be OK to wear thongs in the shower at a caravan park but do you really want to do this in your own home? Keep the area clean with bicarb and white vinegar. Sprinkle bicarb over the surfaces then splash some white vinegar over the top and wipe with a sponge or brush. Then rinse with water. For vertical surfaces, have a tray with some bicarb in it and a bucket with white vinegar in it and use two separate sponges. Begin with the bicarb sponge then press the white vinegar sponge over the bicarb sponge and wipe. Rinse with water.

If you have particularly grimy surfaces, use Gumption. If you like fragrance, add a couple of drops of tea tree oil, lavender oil or eucapytus oil to the rinse water. Don't use eucalyptus oil on anything plastic or painted.

You could also keep a squeegee in the shower recess and give the area a quick wipe after showering to help with cleaning. If you have a shower curtain, leave it stretched open to dry so mould doesn't grow in the crevices.

If you have a separate bath and shower, I suggest having two of everything – from soap to shampoo – so you're not constantly reaching from one area to another, especially when wet! And on the topic of soap, I think each family member should have their own bar of soap in the shower.

If there are several people in your home, wipe tea tree oil over the shower floor with a cloth after each shower to kill germs.

Problem: **Soap scum build-up in soap holder.**
What to use: **Old pair of stockings, warm water.**
How to apply: Scrub the soap scum with an old pair of stockings rolled into a ball and warm water.

Shower screen

As a general rule, it's best not to use abrasives or strong chemicals on any shower screens. If you have a glass shower screen, clean it with bicarb and white vinegar like the rest of the shower. Some shower screens have nylon and wire in between two layers of glass, and problems occur because air cavities are created. This allows moisture to get in and causes either mould or glass cancer on the inside of the screen. It often looks as though you've got soap scum on the screen. I've seen this many times and unfortunately there's not much you can do about it. You can alleviate the scratchiness with sweet almond oil, if you can obtain some, which you rub over the surface and edges. Reapply sweet almond oil every time you clean. If you can't live with the scratchiness, you'll have to buy a new screen or get some glass-etching cream and make the clouds a feature. The other common type of shower screen is made of polycarbonate and should only be cleaned with white vinegar.

Problem:	**Mould in silicone join.**
What to use:	**Oil of cloves, bicarb, white vinegar, old tooth-brush/silicone remover, sharp knife, silicone or candle wax**
How to apply:	First lightly spray the mould with a mixture of a quarter of a teaspoon of oil of cloves in 1 litre of water and leave to dry for 24 hours. To remove the mould detritus sprinkle bicarb over it and then spray with white vinegar. Scrub with an old toothbrush then rinse off with water. If this doesn't work you may need to remove the silicone with a special silicone remover or a very sharp knife. Then replace with new silicone or candle wax.

Shower curtain

Constant moisture and poor ventilation make the shower curtain a prime candidate for mould. Whether it's plastic or nylon, wash the curtain in the washing machine on the cool cycle once a fortnight. To prevent further mildew, add a drop of oil of cloves to the rinse water of the washing machine.

Shower head

If the water in your shower head sprays in different directions, it's likely you've got hard-water fur. If you can see little black prickly things coming out of the nozzle, that's also hard-water fur. Unless you have brass fittings, to get rid of it use descaler. Mix descaler according to the directions on the packet in a bucket or old ice cream container. Hold the container so that the shower head is completely immersed. Keep it there until the solution is absorbed. This should take a few minutes. Then turn on the shower: the black prickles will drop out and go down the drain. For any strays, use a needle to unblock the holes. You can also unscrew the shower head and clean it inside the ice cream container with descaler. Keep brass shower heads clean with equal parts white vinegar and lemon juice applied with an old toothbrush. Brass shower heads are generally big enough to scrub the hard-water fur out.

> **DID YOU KNOW?** Our sense of smell is very powerful, so if you use a fragrance normally associated with food in the bathroom, the smell centre in our brain registers it as wrong. It's best not to use fragrances associated with food, such as cinnamon, apricot or peach, in the bathroom. Lavender is my scent of choice.

TAPS

You always create a good impression if your taps are clean and shiny. Taps can be made of stainless steel, brass, copper, chrome or powder coated. The best way to clean them is with bicarb and white vinegar, except powder-coated taps. Powder coating is a form of plastic that is heat sealed onto the surface of metal to colour it. It often comes in cream, white and black. Don't use abrasives, just wash with soap and water. An old pair of stockings is the easiest way to clean taps. Wrap them around the tap and saw backwards and forwards.

You could also use an old toothbrush to access any hard-to-reach areas. Make sure you clean around the edging of all the drains.

To clean extractor fans
Remove the grill, rinse it under warm water, dry with a towel then replace. Never touch the fan or you could electrocute yourself!

TILES

Clean tiles once a week with bicarb and white vinegar. Have one sponge with bicarb on it and the other with white vinegar on it and put the white vinegar-soaked sponge over the top of the bicarb-coated sponge, then wipe. The grout between the tiles is very porous and retains mildew. To clean it, use bicarb and white vinegar and scrub with an old toothbrush. To inhibit mould, add a couple of drops of oil of cloves to the mixture. You should clean the grout every couple of months to avoid build-up.

There is another way to keep mould under control but you may baulk at this suggestion. Keep a couple of slugs! Slugs will happily eat mould. They sleep during the day so if you create a little house for them, you won't step on them while showering!

MIRROR

When I learned that scuba divers keep their goggles clear by spitting into them, I tested this on the bathroom mirror and found that spit stops the mirror from fogging. Just spit onto a tissue and wipe it over the mirror. If this doesn't appeal to you, write on the mirror with pure soap then polish vigorously with a slightly damp paper towel. I discovered this at an Ideal Home Show where a man was selling 'Magic Mirror Demisting Sticks'. They turned out to be just soap.

HAND BASIN AND VANITY UNIT

Clean the hand basin and vanity with bicarb and white vinegar. Sprinkle bicarb over the surface, then wipe with a white vinegar-soaked sponge. Clean cupboards and shelving the same way. To prevent bottles breaking in your drawers, line the drawers with a thin piece of foam rubber. This cushions any drops and makes cleaning the drawers easier.

Allocate one shelf for each member of the family. Determine a spot on the shelf for each thing you store there and make sure you return items to this spot. It means you won't waste time searching for what you need. No matter how you store toothbrushes, they will always attract bacteria – rinse them before and after cleaning your teeth. Replace them when the bristles start to bend, because if they're not straight, they won't work properly. Store with the bristles facing upwards and try not to let them come into contact with other toothbrushes. If they become contaminated, throw them out or add them to your clean kit. However you store them, make sure you clean the holder and allow it to dry before putting the toothbrushes back in.

HINT

Razors should be cleaned after each use. If you have an electric razor, clean it with a brush and sewing machine oil it each time you use it. Disposable razors should be cleaned by running your fingers from the lubricating strip down the blade, not against the blade, or you'll cut your fingers! If you prefer, use a soft sponge to clean it. It's a good idea to replace them often because bacteria is attracted to them. If you cut yourself a lot when shaving, keep a styptic pencil in the vanity unit. This has an alum base and shrinks blood vessels.

Problem:	**Mildew on vanity cupboard.**
What to use:	**Salt, bucket, hot water, oil of cloves, sponge.**
How to apply:	Dissolve 225 g of salt in a bucket of hot water. Add 2 drops of oil of cloves. Wipe this on the inside of the vanity with a sponge. This will also help to keep insects away.

DID YOU KNOW? Soap for washing your hands should have a slightly higher acidic base to help kill bacteria and cut through grease. I use lemon myrtle soap.

HINT

If you drop foundation make-up on the floor
Blot with a paper towel. Then mix ½ teaspoon of glycerine and ½ teaspoon of washing up liquid and apply to the stain. Massage the mixture into the stain with your fingertips, remove with a paper towel, then a damp cloth. Foundation has a fine grade oil and sticks to everything.

HINT

Toys
Anyone with young children will have an array of toys in the bath. To help with cleaning, and to avoid sitting or stepping on a sharp piece of plastic, keep a toy net in the bathroom. You can easily make your own. Buy some nylon netting, which comes in a variety of colours, from a hardware shop. Attach two large stainless steel curtain rings to either end, then pull the ends together and thread with a cord. Hang the toy net on a hook in the bathroom where it can drain. You could also reuse orange netting bags from the fruit market if there's only a small number of toys – and if orange goes with your bathroom.

TOWELS

I prefer to store towels away from the bathroom because they can get a musty smell from the steam. But if you do store them here, make sure they are kept under a shelf so moisture doesn't drop onto them – and don't roll them up because you will create a mould centre. After using them, towels must be allowed to dry on a towel rack or they'll smell and make you smell as well! Try to get as much air as possible through the towel, so hang it unfolded. If you don't have the space, fold it in two, reversing the fold each day. You can tell which side you've folded by the seam. If you don't have a towel rack, hang the towel on the clothes line. Keep a hand towel near the sink so your bath towel isn't used to dry hands.

Wash towels once a week. Keep them soft by adding bicarb to the wash water and white vinegar to the rinse. Use warm water when washing dark towels to retain the colour.

Clean towel rails, including heated ones, with a cloth that's been wrung out in water.

> The best bathroom mats use a high density towelling that absorbs water and stays stiff so you won't slip. Wash them once a week in the washing machine.

BATHROOM WALLS

Moisture and poor ventilation are generally the reasons painted bathroom walls go mouldy. Leave the window open as much as possible and use ceiling vents. Each time you clean, add 2 drops of oil of cloves to your rinse water and wipe the walls. Oil of cloves will prevent mould growing and makes the walls easier to clean. It also has a nice fresh smell.

'We're repainting our bathroom walls,' reports James. 'At the moment, there's quite a bit of mould on them. Is there anything we can use to stop the mould coming back once we've painted?'

Problem: **Mould on painted walls.**
What to use: **Bicarb, white vinegar, sponge; oil of cloves.**
How to apply: Wipe bicarb and white vinegar over the walls with a sponge before you paint them. Also use a mould inhibitor such as oil of cloves or a proprietary product before and during the painting.

CHAPTER 5:
The Lounge, Dining and Family Rooms

These rooms are all about flow. The lounge flows into the dining room and into the family room, then out onto the patio, around by the barbecue and out into the garden. It's a great way to live, but it means that eating, drinking, playing and socialising are happening all through these spaces. Someone is going to spill their latte on the sofa, an adorable child is going to smear paint over the floor, battalions of muddy shoes are going to mark their path to the TV. Relax! Smile like they do in the cleaning commercials on TV, because we can fix everything!

For many people, there's not a lot of lounging going on in the lounge. In some homes, this area is converted into a playroom for children with toys such as racing car tracks and doll's houses placed smack bang in the middle of the room. Other houses combine all the communal areas of the home – the lounge, dining and family rooms – into a grand living space. And yet other houses have separate lounge and dining rooms, formal spaces that are reserved for special occasions, which may also be the show-off rooms – the places where guests are likely to spend their time. Whatever your arrangement, the cleaning process is similar. Tailor these general instructions to your individual needs!

ASSEMBLE THE CLEAN KIT

beeswax, lavender oil, lemon oil – combined to make furniture polish
bicarb – cleaning agent
cloth – to wipe over surfaces
clutter bucket – to transport displaced items
dusters – to clear dust
furniture polish – to polish furniture
hairdryer – to clean ornaments
insecticide spray – to deter insects

paper towel – to absorb water and polish
small soft paintbrush – to clean ornaments
spray bottle – to hold white vinegar and water
white vinegar – cleaning agent

CLEANING SPECIFIC TO THE THESE ROOMS

Begin with your clutter bucket, putting in it anything that doesn't belong in the room. Place it outside the room. Add a little lemon oil to a soft broom head or a long-handled duster and dust the ceiling and light fittings – the lemon oil will transfer to the dusted surface and inhibit spiders. Then dust the walls with a broom covered in an old T-shirt. Wipe down all paintings, picture frames or wall art, especially along the tops of frames. Wipe light switches and power points with white vinegar on a cloth. Wipe door jambs with either white vinegar or washing up liquid and water on a cloth adding lavender oil for fragrance. Dust over window sills.

Wipe all surfaces including tables with the appropriate cleaner (see later for details on how to clean surfaces). I advise against using silicone-based cleaners as silicone builds up each time you use it, trapping dirt between the layers and, because there's no solvent for it, you can't release that dirt! To clean laminate, use equal parts white vinegar and water on a cloth.

Perspex tables can only be cleaned with washing-up liquid and water. Never use abrasives on Perspex or it will mark (proprietary window cleaners are abrasive).

Don't forget to wipe along shelves. Anything that's a dust magnet, such as knick knacks, bric-a-brac or ephemera needs to be wiped with a cloth that has been tightly wrung out in water. Dust should be blown off fragile ornaments with a hairdryer on a low setting. Loosen any tough spots with a small soft paintbrush then use the hairdryer.

If your fireplace is operational, clean it after each use. To clean the surrounds, simply dust the area with a soft clean cloth. Clean the mantelpiece according to what it's made of. Use diluted white vinegar to clean marble, then rinse with clean water. Wood can be cleaned with a little washing-up liquid, water and an old pair of stockings scrunched into a ball. If there is smoke or soot staining, try cleaning with white vinegar and an old pair of tights first. If that doesn't work, collect some of the ash from the fireplace, mix with water to make a slurry, then wipe over the area. Allow it to dry then rub off with an old pair of pantyhose. To clean the inside cavity of the fireplace, hire a chimney sweep.

Next, sprinkle a small amount of bicarb over the carpet, sofas and soft furnishings. Roughly pat the bicarb through the soft furnishings with your hands to both deodorise and clean any light soil marks. Then vacuum the soft furnishings and the floor. Make sure you remove the cushions on the sofa and chairs and vacuum underneath them.

If you spill something on the sofa, work out what the stain is made of, then use its solvent. Remove protein stains with cold water and soap suds, remove fats with warm water and washing up liquid suds, remove chemicals with their (preferably non-toxic) solvent. You can identify protein stains because they have a dark edging around the stain. Carbohydrate stains are evenly coloured across the stain.

If there are any spider webs around the sofa, remove them and wipe lemon oil on the underside of the sofa. Spiders hate lemon oil and will stay away.

Don't forget to clean bookshelves with the brush head attachment on the vacuum cleaner. Vacuum curtains, pelmets and picture rails with the brush head attachment. Before using the brush head attachment, make sure it's clean. To clean it, wash in water and dry in the sunshine.

Vacuum floors and, if it's a hard floor, wipe over with a cloth that's been wrung out in white vinegar.

SOFA AND FURNITURE CARE

I often sew while sitting on the sofa but learned the hard way not to use the armrest as a pincushion! Vacuum once a week, making sure to clean under and behind cushions. If you're lucky, you might even find some spare change. Cotton, wool or blended sofas can be cleaned with non-toxic upholstery or carpet cleaner. I've found that carpet cleaner is preferable because it's a drier foam and the less water you use the better. Always test a patch first to see if it's colour-fast. Put a damp cloth, such as a white towel, onto a section of the fabric and rub a warm iron over it. If any colour comes off on the towel, it's not colour-fast and you can't use an upholstery or carpet cleaner. Instead, clean with unprocessed wheat bran in a process described later in this chapter or go to a professional cleaner. You can also test colour-fastness by putting white vinegar on a cloth and rubbing the upholstery. If any colour is transferred to the cloth, it's not colour-fast. Just make sure you test in an inconspicuous spot.

Every couple of months, remove all cushions and turn the sofa upside down. Vacuum any insects and discover lost items, as I did with a ring once. If you find spider webs under the sofa, wipe the corners with some lemon oil to deter future spiders. If yours is a house with four-legged friends, get rid of fur and hair by putting on disposable rubber gloves. Then wash your gloved hands with soap and water. This removes the powder from the gloves. Shake your gloved hands dry and drag them over the fur and hair on the sofa or chairs. The water on the gloves makes them statically charged and the rubber draws the fur away. I learned this trick after an Old English sheepdog followed me home. It was the hairiest dog I've ever come across and always seemed to drop white hair on dark colours and black hair on light colours. Also bath your animal regularly.

With food spills, always clean up as much as you can with paper towels, working from the outside to the inside of the spill. Remember to remove protein stains first with a cake of bathroom soap and a little cold water, and then deal with fat stains with detergent suds and a little hot water. If you remove the fats first, you set the proteins and the task becomes so much harder. If in doubt, always treat the stain as though it has protein in it and use cold water first. If they're just grime stains, use wheat bran and white vinegar.

After washing cushion covers, put them back on when they're almost dry but just slightly damp. They'll be easier to put back on because the fibres are relaxed. No need to iron!

To avoid vacuum-cleaner marks on fabric, put an old T-shirt or cloth over the end of the tube or head of the vacuum cleaner and secure with an elastic band. Scotchgarding furniture adds another layer of protection and prevents stains.

 'We recently had our linen-blend sofa cleaned,' says Helen. 'And then we found some dead silverfish. What can we do?'

Problem:	**Silverfish in sofa.**
What to use:	**Cloves.**
How to apply:	The best way to deter silverfish is with whole cloves. Scatter them at the back of and underneath the sofa.

Cotton fabric

Many people ask how to remove pen stains from fabric. The first thing you need to establish is what kind of ink is in the pen, which will be written on the pen. It's either water-based or spirit-based ink or permanent ink.

Problem: Ink stain on fabric.

What to use: Milk, washing up liquid, water.

How to apply: Rot the milk by leaving it in the sun until solids form. The time this takes varies according to the weather and the age of the milk. Place the solids on the stain, leave until you see the ink start to rise up in the solids, then wash the solids out using washing up liquid and water.

Problem: Rust stains on fabric.

What to use: Descaler, water, cotton wool ball, cotton bud/ salt, lemon juice/salt, white vinegar, cloth, water.

How to apply: Only use descaler if you can get to both sides of the fabric, as you must be able to rinse it off. Dilute 1 part descaler to 20 parts water. Hold a cotton wool ball on the non-stained side of the fabric and apply diluted descaler to the rust stain with a cotton bud. You will see the rust loosen from the fibres. Then rinse thoroughly with water. For a natural alternative, put salt on the rust then add lemon juice. Leave it to dry then repeat. It could take a few attempts before the rust shifts. Another option is a salt and white vinegar solution. Mix them together to form a thick paste and apply it to the rust mark. When the rust bleeds into the fabric, rinse with water.

Q: 'My children were playing with lipstick and got some over the fabric ottoman,' reports Magda. 'Can I get it off?'

Problem: Lipstick on fabric.

What to use: Glycerine, cotton wool ball.

How to apply: Put some glycerine on a cotton wool ball and wipe from the outside to the inside of the stain. Just make sure you don't get the fabric too wet.

Q: 'My husband likes to read the newspaper in an armchair. But I've noticed that it has become really grubby on the arms from the newspaper ink. It's covered in a cream cotton fabric. Is there anything I can do?' asks June.

Problem: Dirty marks on fabric.

What to use: White vinegar, sponge, unprocessed wheat bran, handkerchief or muslin cloth/wheat bran, white vinegar, bowl, soft brush.

How to apply: For lighter marks, gently damp the dirty section of the chair with white vinegar on a sponge. Then wrap some bran in a handkerchief or muslin cloth and rub it over the damp section. For dirtier marks, make a bran ball. Put 1 cup of unprocessed wheat bran in a bowl and add white vinegar, 1 drop at a time, until the mixture resembles brown sugar – it should be clumping but not wet. Place the mixture into the toe of a pair of stockings and tie tightly. Rub the stockings across the surface as though using an eraser. The bran ball is preferable to carpet cleaner when giving the couch a spruce up because it's gentler on fabrics. After cleaning, spray with *Scotchgard* (about once a year) to provide the couch with a layer of protection. And if you get lots of grubby marks, consider making or buying removable slipcovers that can be put in the washing machine. Much easier!

Problem: Oily stain on fabric.

What to use: Baby oil, washing up liquid/washing up liquid, water.

How to apply: The higher the carbon content, the more difficult the oil stain is to remove. As a general rule, remove dark oils such as car grease with a dab of baby oil on a cloth followed by washing up liquid massaged in with your fingers. To remove light oils, such as olive oil, massage washing up liquid into the stain with your fingers. If you accidentally used baby oil on a light oil stain, fix by massaging washing up liquid into the stain with your fingers, then rinse in blood-heat water.

Problem: Cigarette smells in furniture.

What to use: Bicarb, wooden spoon, vacuum cleaner.

How to apply: Sprinkle the upholstery with bicarb then beat it with a wooden spoon. Once you've finished beating, vacuum the bicarb off.

Brocade

Brocade is an intricately woven fabric made from any fibre. The weave is very fine so special care must be taken when cleaning it. Use white vinegar and wheat bran as for dirty marks on fabric above to clean it, or go to a professional cleaner.

Q: 'I was lucky enough to inherit my granny's antique chair, which is covered in brocade. But she must have had a leaking hot-water bottle because the chair is covered in water stains. What should I do?' asks Brenda.

Problem:	**Water marks on fabric.**
What to use:	**Sponge, white vinegar, bran, muslin/clean handkerchief, soft brush, vacuum cleaner.**
How to apply:	Dampen the water marks with a sponge soaked in white vinegar, then wrap some bran in muslin or a clean handkerchief and wipe it over the white vinegar. If the stains are really stubborn, you may need to apply the bran directly. Heap it over the white vinegar, brush with a soft brush then vacuum off.

Velvet

In the 1960s, velvet was really fashionable. I used to go to furniture upholsterers and use their offcuts to create clothes, particularly waistcoats. But velvet is one of the hardest fabrics to clean. Start by trying to remove as much fluff as possible. Wear rubber gloves, wash your hands in soapy water, shake dry and rub the gloves over the velvet. The fluff should stick to the gloves. After you've removed as much as possible, give the velvet a light spray with a carpet cleaner. Leave it to dry then vacuum the carpet cleaner off.

Problem:	**Grease stain on velvet.**
What to use:	**Bicarb, bristle brush, vacuum cleaner.**
How to apply:	Sprinkle the stain with bicarb then brush it gently backwards and forwards with a bristle brush, not a nylon brush. Leave it for 10 minutes then vacuum or brush firmly.

Q: 'I've got a water mark on my velvet sofa which has made the velvet bits go all hard and bristly,' says Belinda. 'Can it be repaired?'

Problem:	**Water mark on velvet.**
What to use:	**Bowl, wheat bran, white vinegar, brush, vacuum cleaner.**
How to apply:	In a bowl, mix bran with drops of white vinegar until it's just damp but not clumpy. Then apply the mixture to the water mark with your fingers and leave for a few minutes. Brush the area in circles and leave to dry. Then vacuum the wheat bran.

Problem:	**Bald patch in velvet.**
What to use:	**Matches, stranded cotton or silk, tufting tool.**
How to apply:	First, you need to determine what the velvet is made of. Test a patch along a seam using the head of a hot match. If the fabric smells like burnt hair, it's cotton or silk. If it smells of plastic, it's polyester. Cotton has a matt finish. Silk has a high sheen. Find matching fabric, then use a tufting tool to stab and loop the fibres through the bald patch. (Tufting tools come with easy instructions but practise on a scrap piece of fabric first.) Then trim the cotton or silk threads to the same height as the velvet with sharp scissors. Embroidery or manicure scissors should do the job.

Tapestry

I used to do a lot of tapestries and petit point. The best way to clean tapestry is with dry unprocessed wheat bran. Put a handful into a muslin cloth bag, heat it in the microwave for half a minute, then rub it over the tapestry. The bran will absorb the dirt. You can also apply the bran directly. Firstly, slightly moisten it with white vinegar. Add one drop at a time until it forms clumps like couscous, but not a ball. Sprinkle this across the stain, rub backwards and forwards with a cloth or soft brush, then vacuum it off.

 'I've got a piano stool that is covered in a wool tapestry,' says Shirley. 'It was a wedding gift from my aunt 50 years ago. And after years of use, you can hardly see the flowers any more. Can it be cleaned?'

Problem:	**Dirty tapestry.**
What to use:	**Wheat bran/heavy cotton, woolwash, bucket.**
How to apply:	Try cleaning it with bran as outlined above. If that doesn't work, test it for colour-fastness by soaking a white cloth in white vinegar and applying to a small, less noticeable portion of the tapestry. If any colour comes off, it is not colour-fast. If it is colour-fast, remove the tapestry from the stool and stitch it to a piece of heavy cotton. Hand wash it in 1 teaspoon of woolwash or shampoo added to a bucket of blood-heat water, then completely rinse the piece in blood-heat water before drying it in the shade. You can unstitch the cotton backing or leave it on. Either way, replace the tapestry on the stool while the cotton is still slightly damp because it will have more stretch. If it's not colour-fast, take it to a restorer.

You can make your own woolwash with 2 table-spoons of pure soap flakes, ½ cup of cheap hair conditioner and 2–3 drops of eucalyptus oil. Mix with a little warm water or put into a jar and shake. One teaspoon of this mixture is enough for a bucket of jumpers.

Leather

Clean leather sofas once a week with either saddle soap or leather conditioner. Keep a dedicated cloth in a plastic zip-lock bag for this purpose. Never use water to clean leather because it stiffens it. And always secure a cloth or T-shirt over the vacuum-cleaner head to prevent scratches in the leather. Never use toothpaste on stains as it can leave dry, rough or bleached spots.

Problem:	**Dog and cat scratches in dark brown leather.**
What to use:	**Walnut/shoe cream, cloth, leather conditioner/camphor, mothballs and holder, lavender oil or lavender bags.**
How to apply:	Remove the walnut from its shell, if it has one, and cut it in half. Then rub the cut walnut over the scratch so that its oils coat the scratch. Leave for 1 hour for the colour to cure. If the sofa isn't brown leather, choose an appropriately coloured shoe cream but not shoe polish or wax. Apply the shoe cream with a cloth. It only feeds the areas that need it. After that, apply leather conditioner with a cloth to soften.

To prevent more scratches, scatter camphor at the back of the sofa, and underneath the cushions, to deter a cat. You could also tuck a mothball holder between the cushions. Use lavender oil or lavender bags behind the seat cushions to deter a dog.

Cane, bamboo and wicker furniture

Cane tends to be a very popular restoration item. Our family has a
set of early Victorian cane baby furniture that has been passed from
family to family. The best way to clean cane, bamboo and wicker is
to mix 2 teaspoons of bicarb in 1 litre of water and rub it over the
furniture with a sponge, then rinse. Dab some baby oil on a cloth to
polish.

How to fix a hole in cane furniture

Use some matching or similar cane that is longer than the hole
you're repairing. Make it into single canes and soak them in hot
water. Reweave the cane starting where the original cane is still
solid. Don't cut away the old pieces until it's been rewoven. Tuck
the ends in and down at the end of each row. If you're replacing
a seat, tack some outdoor canvas to the underside of the chair for
reinforcement. Use spray paint rather than a brush to paint the
cane. Re-varnish with shellac in a spray bottle rather than enamel
or polyurethane. One of the nicest things about cane furniture is its
ability to flex and mould to the sitter. That's the squeaking sound
you hear. Enamel and polyurethane weld the cane together as a
solid block and you lose that comfort. They are also hard to
remove if you decide you don't like the colour or if they get
damaged. Shellac comes in a range of colours and is removable
if you decide you don't like the colour.

Metal-framed furniture

Aluminium, chrome and stainless-steel furniture can be cleaned with
white vinegar and water on a cloth. If it's very dirty, use white vinegar
with bicarb. Clean wrought iron with bicarb and white vinegar then
wipe it either with baby oil or sewing machine oil. If it's painted,

clean it with washing up liquid and water. To create a high sheen and to prevent rust and corrosion, clean metals with car polish.

Wooden furniture

One of the great things about being a restorer is learning what all the expensive cleaning products are made of. I discovered that furniture polishes are based either on lemon peel and beeswax, orange peel and beeswax, canuba wax or silicone. Now you can make polish yourself! Be aware, though, that different wooden finishes require different kinds of cleaning.

If the wood on your new furniture is too shiny, wipe a mixture of talcum powder and cornflour over the surface with a piece of silk. If the wood is scratched and you would like to soften the mark, dampen the silk with white vinegar first. Damp silk is more abrasive.

Lacquer is made with layers of rice paper, plant resin, mineral dyes and vegetable gum and is difficult to keep in good condition. It should never be kept at less than 30 per cent humidity or it will dry out and crack. If it's in a dry spot, put a large bowl of water under it or place potted plants around it to create your own mini tropical climate. Use a damp cloth, never wet, to clean it. Never use washing up liquid and see a specialist restorer for any significant problems. Small chips in black items can be covered with black boot polish.

Laminate can be cleaned with bicarb and white vinegar.

Polyurethane can be cleaned with a damp cloth. For very dirty surfaces, use washing up liquid. Keep water away from scratched surfaces. To repair any bubbling, inject with a syringe under each bubble a small quantity of 1 part Unibond PVA and 20 parts water. Put cling film over the bubble and weight it with a book or block. Leave for some time to allow it to dry.

Clean **shellac** with a good quality, silicone-free furniture polish or beeswax.

Varnish should be cleaned with a good quality, silicone-free furniture polish. If you have oily or grimy patches, scatter damp tea leaves over the stain and allow the tannins to break down and absorb the grime. Then polish with silicone-free furniture polish or beeswax.

Veneer should be cleaned with a good quality, silicone-free furniture polish applied with a soft cloth. Keep away from direct sunlight or the edges will lift.

Problem:	**Scratches in wood.**
What to use:	**Baby oil/coloured wax crayons, soft dry cloth.**
How to apply:	Baby oil is great for taking out small scratches and stains in woodwork. For larger scratches, use coloured crayons that are made of wax. Mix colours to match your wood and draw over the scratch. Then lightly polish with a soft dry cloth.

Problem:	**Scratches on polyurethane.**
What to use:	**Cornflour, silk bag, cloth.**
How to apply:	Put cornflour into a silk bag and dampen it so that the cornflour works its way into the silk. This will act as a mild cutting agent. Rub the bag over the scratches then polish any residue off with a dry cloth.

Problem:	**Heat marks.**
What to use:	**Beeswax, lemon peel/bicarb, olive oil, cloth.**
How to apply:	If the damage isn't too bad, use some warmed beeswax applied with the yellow side of the lemon peel (remove the flesh first). If it's quite damaged, use a mixture of 1 part bicarb and 1 part olive oil, paint it onto the mark, leave for a few minutes, then polish it off with a cloth before polishing normally.

Problem: Small amount of woodworm in furniture.
What to use: WD-40.
How to apply: Place the skinny nozzle of the WD-40 can on each hole and give a quick squirt.

Problem: White stain on dark wood.
What to use: Walnut juice/toothpaste.
How to apply: The amount you need depends on how big the stain is. Cut an unshelled walnut in half and rub the walnut over the white stain to darken it. One of the oldest ways to remove water rings from shellac is with toothpaste. Toothpaste is a mild abrasive and creates tiny holes over the water spot. When you wax it, the wax gets in behind where the stain was and fills up the air cavities.

Q: 'I hosted a dinner party the other night which went really well except candle wax dropped onto the dining table,' says Jane. 'How can I get it off without damaging the wood?'

Problem: Candle wax on wood.
What to use: Ice, soft scraper, silk cloth, paper towel, hairdryer, rubber gloves.
How to apply: Harden the wax with ice, then remove as much as possible with a soft scraper. Make sure you scrape along the grain of the timber. Rub the rest of the wax off with a damp silk cloth. Make sure it's real silk. If the wax has dripped onto unsealed wood, remove as much as possible with the silk cloth, then press a paper towel over the wax and heat with a hairdryer, keeping the paper towel over the

wax as you dry. The wax will be absorbed by the
paper towel. Keep changing the paper towel until
the wax is completely removed. Wear rubber
gloves so you don't get burnt fingers. Use a
stop–start method so you don't overheat the wood
and allow it to cool between each try.

Q: 'I've got some wax on a French-polished table,'
says Carole. 'Can I get it off without ruining the
polish?'

Problem:	**Wax on polished wood.**
What to use:	**Warmed silk.**
How to apply:	You must use pure silk. Warm the silk first by wetting it and then placing it in the microwave. Then rub it over the wax. You can use a dry piece of silk but this will take longer to remove the wax.

Problem:	**Veneer lifting or bubbling.**
What to use:	**Syringe, Unibond PVA, water, cloths.**
How to apply:	Fill a syringe with 1 part Unibond PVA to 20 parts water. The mixture should be the consistency of runny cream. Inject a small quantity into the centre of the bubble or underneath the edge of the piece that is lifting, then press down. Place a weight, such as a heavy book, on it while it dries. (Use a piece of cling film to protect the book.) To cover the injection hole mark, rub it with a hot damp cloth, leave it to dry and then polish with a dry cloth.

Problem:	**Sticking drawers.**
What to use:	**Soap or candle wax/spirit level, cardboard or block of wood, glue.**
How to apply:	Rub the soap or candle wax along the runners. If this doesn't work, your chest of drawers may not be level. Check by using a spirit level, and if it's not even, put some cardboard or a block of wood under one of the legs. Also check that the joints of the drawer itself are secure. Re-glue them if they are loose.

Tables

If you have a valuable wooden dining table, I strongly suggest using a table protector to guard against scratches. Use heat-resistant placemats and have extra mats for the centre of the table when serving. Using tablecloths will cut down on mess and help with your cleaning.

French polish is created by layering very thin coatings of shellac either on wood or papier-mâché. Clean it with a non-silicone-based furniture polish. Try not to use water near French polish because it will whiten the surface.

DID YOU KNOW? Mixing beeswax, lavender oil and lemon oil on a cloth is a great wood cleaner. Antique shops often use this combination. To create the cleaning cloth, place the cloth in a microwave-safe bowl and add 1 drop of lavender oil, 1 drop of lemon oil and 1 tablespoon of beeswax on top. Warm it in the microwave in 10-second bursts until the beeswax melts. The cloth will be impregnated with the mixture and is ready to use. Store it in a zip-lock plastic bag.

HINT

To repair a heat mark on a table

Heat marks appear as a white ring on your table. To repair a French polish finish, use beeswax applied with a piece of lemon peel. If the table is very damaged, use a mixture of 1 part bicarb and 1 part olive oil, paint it onto the mark, leave for a few minutes, then polish it off with a cloth. Polish normally.

Be very careful with polyurethane surfaces because, if you scratch them, you'll have to reseal them. If the scratch has penetrated through to the wood, you'll have to reseal the area, which is a big job. If this is the case, seek the advice of a professional.

If heat has bubbled the surface, for French polish, see a restorer. For a polyurethane finish, fill a syringe with 1 part Aquadhere to 20 parts water. The mixture should be the consistency of runny cream. Inject a small quantity into the centre of the bubble then press down. Place a weight, such as a heavy book, on it while it dries, using a piece of cling film to protect the underside of the book.

CHAIRS

Don't forget to wipe chairs because they are great dust collectors – and don't forget to clean the legs as well.

Clean **vinyl** with white vinegar and water mixture then rinse with a damp cloth.

Wash loose **fabric** covers or removable cushions regularly, either by hand or in the washing machine. If you can, have two sets of covers so you can replace them immediately. If you like, use different colours to change the whole of the area. Upholstered chairs should be vacuumed or brushed thoroughly with a lint- or clothes-brush. If they're stained, mix unprocessed wheat bran and white vinegar until it forms clumps and rub it over the stain. Leave to dry, then vacuum.

Leather should be treated with leather conditioner. For scratches, if the leather is brown, rub a cut walnut along the scratch. For other colours, use shoe cream along the scratch.

Wood should be cleaned with a small amount of cider white vinegar, water and a damp cloth. Shellac or French polish should be cleaned with a good non-silicone furniture polish.

Plastic should be cleaned with a cloth wrung out in water. For stubborn stains, use washing-up liquid applied with a cloth. Minor scratches can be treated with a small amount of glycerine on a cloth.

The best way to clean **stainless steel** is with bicarb and white vinegar. Mix them together on a sponge and wipe over the chair. Then wipe with a cloth that's been wrung out in water. For scratches, apply a dab of Gumption to a sponge and wipe over the scratch. Then apply bicarb and white vinegar and clean with a cloth.

Clean **chrome** with a cloth and a little washing up liquid and water or white vinegar.

 'We recently had a powercut and had to resort to using candles,' says Janet. 'But my son accidentally knocked over one of the candles and now there's red wax all over a tapestry chair. Can it be fixed?'

Problem:	**Candle wax on tapestry.**
What to use:	**Plastic knife or wooden ice-block stick, paper towel, hairdryer.**
How to apply:	Try and remove as much wax as possible by delicately prising it away with a plastic knife or wooden ice-block stick. For any remaining wax, place some paper towel over it, then apply heat from a hairdryer. The wax should be absorbed by the

paper towel. Keep replacing the paper towel until all the wax is removed. To remove the red colouring, use sunlight. Put the chair outside in the sun and, except for the waxed area, cover it. The staining will fade in sunlight. If you can't put the chair in the sun, hire an ultraviolet light, cover the non-stained part of the chair with an old sheet or towel then aim the light over the stained area. Check it every 2 hours until the stain has gone.

TABLETOPS

Glass

Never use furniture polish on glass and see a restorer for scratches.

Marble

 'I've got water marks from leaving cups of tea on my marble-top table,' reveals Jocelyn. 'Can they be fixed?'

Problem:	Water marks on marble.
What to use:	Bicarb, white vinegar, water, soft brush.
How to apply:	Sprinkle bicarb over the stain, then mix 1 part white vinegar to 5 parts water and sprinkle it over the bicarb. When the mixture fizzes, rub with a soft brush.

TABLECLOTH STAINS

Q: 'I've got a policy of using my lovely things,' says Maria. 'We had a barbecue the other day and I used my white damask tablecloth. Now it's got sausage grease and tomato sauce over it. Can the stains be removed?'

Problem:	**Grease and tomato stains on tablecloth.**
What to use:	**Vanish.**
How to apply:	Tomato sauce fades in sunshine. You could also soak the stain in Vanish. The sausage grease will also come off with Vanish. If you're using good linen in vulnerable situations, buy some heavy-grade plastic from the hardware store to cover it and use a hairdryer to mould the plastic over the tablecloth. Be careful not to keep the hairdryer in one spot for too long or the plastic will melt.

Problem:	**Red-wine stain on tablecloth.**
What to use:	**Bicarb, sponge, white vinegar, cloth/glycerine.**
How to apply:	For fresh stains, sprinkle some bicarb over the area then sponge with white vinegar. If the stain has set, rub bicarb in circles using a cloth dampened with vinegar. For any hard set stains, soak in glycerine before removing the stain normally.

Q: 'One of my dinner guests misjudged the distance between the gravy boat and his plate,' says Carole. 'Now I've got a lovely brown stain on the tablecloth. What should I do?'

Problem: Gravy stain on tablecloth.

What to use: Soap, cold water, hot water.

How to apply: Gravy contains proteins so you must remove them first with soap and cold water. Gravy also contains fat, which you remove with soap and hot water. Just make sure you clean with cold water first or you'll set the stain.

CHINA/ORNAMENTS

These may be worth a lot of money, have sentimental value or simply be a decorating touch. A little attention is often the best approach with ornaments, particularly because dust can cause surfaces to craze. Whether they're clean or dirty, china pieces should be cleaned every six months. Keep a small container of water in display cabinets so the pieces don't dry out, and never put your cabinet against an exterior wall because heat or cold will come through. A constant temperature is best for china. Dust with a hairdryer on a low setting and use a small paintbrush for difficult-to-reach areas. Secure items vulnerable to bumping by putting Blu-Tack underneath them.

Brass should be cleaned using a non-toxic proprietary cleaner or my preferred choice of cleaner, bicarb and white vinegar. If you're coating it, use shellac because it can be removed more easily. Be aware that brass will tarnish even after being coated but the coating will help it last a little longer.

Bronze should be cleaned with a damp soapy cloth, but never rub bronze or you'll remove the patina.

China should be dusted with a hairdryer on a low setting and use a small paintbrush for those difficult-to-reach areas. Wash every six months in blood-heat water and dry thoroughly with a hairdryer. If very dirty, add a little washing up liquid to the water except if the item has non-china elements, such as lace or paper. Never soak china.

Clay ornaments should be vacuumed and dusted regularly. Never soak because clay absorbs moisture. If you wash, do so quickly and dry thoroughly so you don't lift the glaze.

Cloisonné is enamel fused into small wire pockets on the outside of a bronze, brass or copper vessel. Clean it with white vinegar and water. Never use soaps because it will tarnish.

Embroidery, where possible, should be kept out of direct sunlight. Keep it covered and inside cabinets. Hand wash gently if it's colour-fast. If not, take it to a restorer or good dry cleaner.

Ephemera should be kept as flat as possible under glass or in cabinets. Spray fabric with non-toxic surface insecticide spray to keep insects away.

Fabrics should be treated as you would your best table linen. Keep them well dusted and, where possible, vacuum.

Ivory can be cleaned with sweet almond oil applied with a cloth.

Lace should be hand washed in pure soap and rinsed very well. Glue medical gauze underneath a hole to hold it until you're ready to repair it properly. Embroider over the gauze in the same pattern as the lace and trim away any excess gauze.

Paper must be kept dust free and out of direct sunlight. Wash carefully with a slightly damp cloth. Just dab rather than wipe the paper. If in doubt, use a restorer or conservator.

Silver can be cleaned using bicarb and white vinegar. Polish with unprocessed wheat bran.

Tinware can be wiped with warm soapy water and then dried thoroughly with a rag dampened with sewing machine oil. This will prevent rust. If the tin does rust, apply WD-40 with a cloth. To stop insects eating paper labels on tinware, wipe the labels with a damp tea bag.

Wood can, if it's sealed, be cleaned using a good silicone-free furniture polish. If it's unsealed, clean with furniture oil.

Q:

'My daughter brought home some copper Buddha heads from Thailand,' says Katie. 'We sprayed them with a surface spray to get rid of any bugs, and black spots formed from the spray. Can we fix them?'

Problem:	**Tarnished metal.**
What to use:	**Bicarb, white vinegar, cloth.**
How to apply:	Make a paste with 1 part bicarb and 1 part white vinegar and apply it to the tarnish marks with a cloth. Don't get it on other surfaces or it will scratch. Allow the paste to dry then buff it off with a clean, dry cloth.

FIREPLACES

If your fireplace is operational, clean it after each use. To clean the surrounds, simply dust the area. To clean grime from anything except wooden surfaces, use white vinegar.

Q:

'I've got smoke on the brickwork to the side of my fireplace,' says Jim. 'How can I get it off?'

Problem:	**Soot stains around the fireplace.**
What to use:	**Water, ash, cloths, bicarb, white vinegar/ Gumption.**
How to apply:	Add water to some powdered ash from the fireplace to create a slurry, or thin paste, and apply it to the stain with a cloth. Then wash with bicarb and white vinegar. For light stains, combine ash with Gumption and wipe over with a cloth.

Problem:	**Candle soot stains on the wall.**
What to use:	**Vacuum cleaner, ash, sponges, soap, white vinegar, water.**
How to apply:	Candle soot is very greasy, so vacuum any loose particles then rub the soot with a small amount of ash on a dry sponge. Then wipe a little bit of soap onto the soot with another sponge. The soap picks up the last small pieces of soot. Finally, wipe down the surface with another sponge damped in white vinegar and water.

HEATERS

Heaters are more efficient if they're dust free, clean and shiny. Clean and polish reflector plates at the back of the heater with bicarb and white vinegar. This will also get rid of rust. If you have a gas or kerosene heater and are irritated by the fumes, place a saucepan of water beside the heater as this will absorb them. Add a slice of onion to the water with kerosene heaters to help absorb the smells.

ENTERTAINMENT SYSTEMS

The main enemies of entertainment systems are insects and moisture.

Don't use washing up liquid on television screens, plasma screens and the exterior of most entertainment systems because it will leave smear marks. Proprietary brand equipment cleaners that are antistatic are available – check for non-toxic versions if possible. Vacuum all the vents at the back of the system using the brush head of the vacuum cleaner. Wipe the back of all electrics with a cloth sprayed with surface insecticide spray to keep insects away. When they're not in use, close all the doors and compartments of entertainment systems to stop dust getting in. Remove dust from difficult-to-reach areas with a camera puffer brush.

VCR heads should be cleaned using a high-quality video head cleaner or take them to a repairer. Store VHS tapes vertically like a book so you don't stretch the tape.

DVDs should be stored flat or they buckle. Wipe them with a DVD cleaner regularly. CDs should be cleaned using a CD cleaner and cloth if they are sticking.

Have a designated spot for remote controls, which seem to be multiplying. Clean them with a damp cloth. If gunk has accumulated between the buttons, clean between them with a cotton bud.

> **HINT**
> Electronic equipment works better when the vents are clean. Dust them regularly and make sure electronic equipment is kept clean the right way!

Q: 'My girlfriend had a candle burning on top of the entertainment unit and wax dropped onto the fabric cover of the speaker on the TV. Can I get it out?' asks Mark.

Problem:	Wax on fabric.
What to use:	Ice, plastic scraper, pins, tissues, hairdryer.
How to apply:	If possible, take the speaker cover off. Then put ice on the wax and remove as much as possible with a plastic scraper. Next pin tissues to the waxy side of the speaker, turn the cover over and use a hairdryer on the back of the cover. This warms the wax up and the tissues absorb it. If you can't remove the speaker cover, place a tissue over the wax and use

the hairdryer to melt the wax from the front side. The tissue will then absorb most of it. Keep replacing the tissue until all the wax is absorbed. So you don't overheat the fabric, use a stop–start method.

BOOKS AND BOOKSHELVES

Clean bookshelves once a week with a duster, or vacuum with the brush head. To stop books becoming mildewy, sprinkle silicone crystals along the back of the bookshelf or wipe the back of the bookshelf with oil of cloves.

Many books are susceptible to UV rays so try to keep them in a shaded area. If your books are discoloured at the top of the page, it means they were cut at too hot a level on cheap paper. You may also find yellowing on either side of photographic paper, which means it's not acid-free. To prevent damp in your books, keep silicone crystals nearby. One bag per shelf should be enough. Doing this will also cut down on cleaning because damp books collect more dust than dry books. If possible, have a shelf over the top of books to collect dust. Vacuum once a week.

> DID YOU KNOW? If you get grease on a book, cover the spot above and underneath with blotting paper and iron over it with a warm iron. If the stain remains, wipe two pieces of blotting paper with a little washing up liquid, place them above and underneath the stain then press the page firmly with a very cool iron. It's the pressure, not the heat, that shifts the remaining oil.

 Q: 'I've got cockroach droppings all over my books,' says George. 'How can I get rid of them?'

Problem:	**Cockroach droppings on books.**
What to use:	**Vacuum cleaner, bicarb, old toothbrush; salt.**
How to apply:	Vacuum first, then shut the book tight with the spine facing away from your hand. Sprinkle bicarb along the edges and rub with an old toothbrush. To prevent cockroaches returning, pile a bed of salt around the feet of the bookshelf.

Q:

'How can you get rid of awful smells in old books?' asks Graeme.

Problem:	**Smelly books.**
What to use:	**Talcum powder.**
How to apply:	This is a very tedious process. Dust a page with talcum powder, then leave it in the sun for no more than three minutes or the UV rays will affect the paper. Clear the talcum powder, turn the page, apply more talcum powder, leave in the sun, remove the powder, and so on ... for the whole book!

Q:

'I've got brown marks in my books,' says Sue. 'What should I do?'

Problem:	**Brown marks in books.**
What to use:	**This is called foxing or book worm and is a job for a professional conservator.**

DECANTERS

I used to make wine at home and will never forget the day I mistook some Dettol for homemade brew. My throat had a menthol flavour for some time! It's best not to leave alcohol in your decanters for more than a day because it causes white cloudy smears or glass cancer. Spirits should be stored in screw-top bottles and decanted just for the evening. Decanters are best washed in warm water and oven dried. To oven dry, turn your oven on to a very low heat then place the decanter in the oven, turn the oven off and leave. Never put direct heat, such as from a hairdryer, on a decanter as you risk cracking the crystal.

TRAYS

Trays are a great invention. Use silver cleaner to clean silver trays and a damp cloth to clean other trays.

Q: 'I've got a dull grey shadow on a silver tray,' reports Sue. 'Can I get rid of it?'

Problem:	**Shadow on silver tray.**
What to use:	**White toothpaste, silver polish, cloths.**
How to apply:	There are a couple of possible explanations for this. Some trays have nickel silver on the inside and electroplated silver coating on the outside. The silver coating may be wearing thin and exposing the core. Another explanation is that the tray may have been repaired with a different quality silver which is ageing at a different rate. To remove the shadow, wipe white toothpaste over it then clean with a good quality silver polish. Make sure you wash all the silver polish off and then polish with a dry cloth.

Q: 'What's the best way to clean a silver-plated tray?' asks Bill.

Problem:	**Cleaning silver-plated tray.**
What to use:	**Bicarb, white vinegar, cloths/unprocessed wheat bran, white vinegar, cloths.**
How to apply:	Sprinkle bicarb over the tray like icing sugar, then splash white vinegar over the top. Rub over the tray with a damp cloth before polishing it with a dry cloth. You can also mix wheat bran and white vinegar to form a paste and rub it over the silver. Wipe off with a damp cloth then a dry cloth.

ASHTRAYS

The best way to clean ashtrays is with cigarette ash. With a damp cloth, rub ash over the ashtray and then wash in washing up liquid and water.

> ### Create your own air freshener
> Mix ½ teaspoon of vanilla essence, cinnamon oil or eucalyptus oil with a couple of drops of washing up liquid into a spray bottle filled with water. Or put some bicarb in a saucer with a couple of drops of your favourite essential oil and mix well. This will absorb odours and freshen the room. Never use eucalyptus oil if you're spraying painted surfaces or plastic because it will strip them!

CLOCKS

Heirloom and antique clocks should be cleaned by a professional. One of the best ways to maintain your mantle clock is to place an oily cloth inside the sounding box. Use baby oil or sewing machine oil. The dust and rust from the clock movements will fall to the cloth and stick rather than flying around and damaging the workings of the clock. The exterior should be cared for according to what it's made of. Never clean keys with silver or brass cleaner. Just wipe them with an oily rag. No clock should ever sit against the wall as air needs to circulate around it. And always make sure clocks are level.

PIANOS

Most pianos are made of wood and are best cared for with a good furniture polish. Piano keys can be made of plastic, ivory or ivorite. You can tell which is which by the lines in the keys. Plastic keys have no lines. Ivory has slightly uneven lines. Ivorite keys have even lines. Clean plastic keys with glycerine. Ivory keys can be cleaned with sweet almond oil. If the keys are really dirty, use a small quantity of toothpaste mixed with water and apply carefully with a cotton bud. Then apply the sweet almond oil, which will protect the ivory from cracking.

FLOWERS AND POT PLANTS

When I was younger, my job was to arrange flowers for the house. We had fresh flowers in every room. Cut flowers will last longer if you trim their stems just before putting them in water. They will also last longer if you maintain the water level in the vase. Do this by adding ice cubes to the vase every morning and night.

With daisies and soft-leaf plants, trim excess foliage and add a pinch of salt and sugar to the water. This makes the flowers last longer and stops the water from smelling. To keep English violets longer, immerse the whole violet in water for about two minutes and then place in a vase. For roses, put a piece of copper in the water. Rescue wilting roses by trimming the stems and filling the vase with chilled water up to the bract or throat of the rose.

To prevent native flower stems going furry, put a small piece of charcoal in the water. Proprietary products are available as well. Remove the stamens from lilies before putting them in the vase because they cause stains.

Artificial flowers

Plastic, fabric, silk and felt flowers can be dusted regularly with a hairdryer on the cool setting. To clean paper flowers, hold them upside down and lightly shake. Help retain their colour by keeping them away from sunlight and deter insects by placing two cloves in a small green bag and attaching it to the stem. (Try to use a matching green so the bag is camouflaged.)

 Q: 'My daughter just got married and I'd like to dry her wedding bouquet,' says Merle. 'It's made of coloured roses and tulips.'

Problem:	**Drying flowers.**
What to use:	**Bowl, sand, hairdryer, cloves.**
How to apply:	Remove all florist wire, plastic and ribbons. Then place the bouquet upside down in a bowl slightly bigger than the bouquet. Slowly add sand to the bowl. As you do, vibrate the flowers so the sand gets inside all the petals. Try not to bend or damage the petals. When the bouquet is completely covered in sand, put the bowl in the microwave for one-minute bursts until the stems go woody. You can also use the oven on the lowest possible temperature for about three hours. A woody stem indicates that the bouquet is ready. Then let the sand cool before pouring it out. Don't touch the sand while it's hot.

Replace the wires and ribbons. Dried flowers can be cleaned with a hairdryer on the cool setting. Keep insects away with a couple of cloves.

Vases

Vases can be tricky to clean, particularly the big narrow ones. If you're having difficulty removing dirt, cover the stain in baby oil and leave it for a couple of hours. Then remove the oil with either a paintbrush or a bamboo skewer with chewed ends. Make sure the ferrule, or metal part, of the paintbrush is covered so you don't scratch the vase. To access those hard-to-reach areas, create a curl in the end of a bamboo skewer and work it into the area.

> **DID YOU KNOW?** If there's heavy plant matter stuck in the base of a vase, use bicarb and white vinegar. If that doesn't work, add coarse salt and white vinegar and shake. Then rinse and allow to dry.

Indoor plants

It's best not to keep indoor plants near radios, TVs or other electrical equipment. Plants don't like electromagnetic fields, and electrical equipment doesn't like water. An economical way to clean indoor plants that like water on their leaves is to stand them in the shower with a fine mist. Have a shower yourself as a small amount of soap keeps plants healthy.

 Q: 'I've got ants making anthills in my pot plants,' says Cynthia. 'How can I get rid of them?'

Problem:	**Ants in pot plants.**
What to use:	**Hot water.**
How to apply:	Wherever possible, find the source of the ants and pour boiling water on the nest rather than using poisons.

STUDY/OFFICE EQUIPMENT

Every home should have a study or an office, even if it's just a chair and a cupboard. Having one designated spot for papers and documents speeds up your cleaning because you're less likely to have them strewn around the house. I also try to keep my pens and pencils in this spot, although my daughter constantly moves them all around the house. If you keep them in one spot, you minimise ink stains and can always find a pen when you need one.

This is another place where the enemies are dust, insects and moisture. Vacuum often using the brush head attachment of the vacuum cleaner. Ventilate equipment well.

Computers

Computers can be cleaned in a couple of ways. For light cleans, use a warm-water damp cloth. Never use a wet cloth because the ports can corrode – and don't even approach the ports with a damp cloth! For dirty surfaces, apply some antistatic CD spray to a cloth and wipe it over all the surfaces, including the venting hole. Never spray directly onto the computer. Other specialised cleaners are also available. To deter insects, spray non-toxic surface insecticide spray on a rag and wipe the back of the computer with it. Keep computers ventilated by placing them at least 10 centimetres away from any wall. It's fine to use your vacuum cleaner to get at dirt outside the computer but never use it inside the computer because it creates static electricity and could ruin it. You can vacuum the vent holes.

Mouse

You know it's time to clean the mouse when it becomes sticky and hard to manoeuvre. The latest ones are optical and can't be pulled apart but you can clean the case by wiping with a cloth dampened with white vinegar. Make sure you clean the track wheel.

Keyboard

As for cleaning keyboards, so many people eat near them that it's not unusual for crumbs to lodge under the keys. You can turn it upside down and gently shake it, use your vacuum cleaner or compressed air in a can applied through a nozzle. I use my airbrush compressor. To clean keyboard keys, use cotton buds dampened with a little water.

Fax

Clean faxes with a warm-water damp cloth on the outside.

Photocopier

The photocopier is cleaned in the same way as the fax. For excess toner on the photocopier, put on rubber gloves and use a damp cloth to wipe away the toner. Put the cloth into a plastic bag and throw it out as it will stain anything it touches. For mechanical repairs, consult a professional.

DID YOU KNOW? If you spill toner, clean it by lightly dampening a bar of soap with water then dab it on the spill. The toner fragments will stick to the soap as though it were sticky tape. Rinse the bar of soap and repeat this process until you've removed as much as possible, then apply rotten milk solids to the remaining stain. Once all the toner ink is absorbed, remove the rotten milk with soap and a little water on a cloth.

Telephone

Telephones are best cleaned with glycerine on a cloth. Never use alcohol-based chemicals or eucalyptus oil on telephones because they'll affect the plastic. I clean the phone with a small amount of white vinegar and water on a cloth. For the area between the buttons, which is difficult to access, use a cotton bud dipped in white vinegar. Don't forget to clean the phone cord. Start at the receiver, cover the cord with your cleaning cloth and pinch it between your finger and thumb. Then pull the cloth all the way to the end of the cord.

Papers

There are many ways to organise your papers, family photographs, bills, letters and documents. Many people use a filing cabinet to organise these items. Others have trays and some people find that old shoe boxes do the job. You could even recycle old cereal boxes for storage but spray them with insecticide first because insects are attracted to cardboard.

I sort my bills and store them vertically with removable hooks. Each hook keeps a different bill. When the bill is paid, I staple the receipt to it or write the receipt number on it so I can see at a glance which bills have been paid and which ones need to be paid. Having papers hanging vertically means they don't collect dust and don't take up much room – and it's easier to sort through a stack of vertical papers than a pile on a table. One thing to be careful of is receipts using ink that fades – keep them out of sunlight.

Air conditioners and fans

Be careful with air conditioners. I'm a fuss-pot because I know how easy it is for nasties to breed in them. The main thing is to make sure that the air intake is clean. Remove and clean the filter according to the manufacturer's instructions. Some need to be flushed with water and dried in the sunshine. Others just need to have the dust removed from them. If you do this once a week, it won't become a chore. When you wipe the air conditioner, add lavender oil to the cloth to both scent the room and deter insects. Change air conditioner pipes once a year.

HINT

Fans collect dust when they move because they create a static charge. Because dust is so light and oppositely charged, it's attracted to the fan blades and collects grease and makes a horrible mess. If you don't clean fan blades regularly, they'll accumulate an absorbent felt of dust that will go furry. Clean them with either a feather or fabric duster. If your fan is in a sealed unit, unscrew the cover and dust the fan blades. It will work more efficiently and won't spread dust. Dust them regularly and make sure electronic equipment is kept clean the right way!

Whiteboards

Q: 'I want to remove permanent pen from my white-board,' says Eric. 'What's your advice?'

Problem: Removing permanent pen from a whiteboard.
What to use: Perfume, cotton wool ball.
How to apply: Dab some perfume onto a cotton wool ball and wipe over the pen marks.

> **HINT**
>
> **To remove ink stains**
> On soft furnishings – apply rotten milk solids until the ink bleeds into it. Then clean with a little soap and water. To rot milk, simply leave some full-cream milk in the sun until it goes lumpy. The time it takes for the milk to go off will vary, and it will smell off before it goes off. You must wait until the mixture is lumpy before using.

CHAPTER 6:
Floors, Walls and Windows

If you're not spilling stuff on your floors or walls then you're not living. Kids running around, friends over for coffee or a Sunday barbecue, pets traipsing muck over the house . . . This is the stuff of life and, like life, it's messy. Wine will be spilt, greasy sausages will be dropped and wax will drip. However, you can fix all these problems and never have to cry over spilt milk again.

FLOORS

Floors are probably the most susceptible part of the house to dirt, spills and stains. Sweep or vacuum the floors in preparation for mopping. I like to mop floors with a dampened old T-shirt wrapped around a broom head and secured by elastic bands – brooms are much better than mops at getting into corners. The temperature of your mopping water will vary according to the surface. Use cold water on cork, wood, old lino or any absorbent surface. Other surfaces can withstand hot water, which helps break down fats. Add 240 ml of white vinegar to the water to make the surface non-slip.

One of my tricks if someone's about to visit and my hard floors are looking a bit dirty is simply to dampen an old T-shirt in water, wrap it around a broom head and run it over the floor.

Wood and cork

Before you throw your old tea leaves out, lightly scatter them over your sealed wooden floors! Yes, tea is a great way to clean them. Just make sure the tea leaves are damp, not wet. Then vacuum them up immediately. It's a tip I learned from my grandmother who loved drinking tea as well. You can use tea bags instead by tying them behind your broom and then sweeping. After vacuuming, add a couple of drops of your favourite essential oil (I use lavender) to a bucket of water and wipe the floor with a mop. If you don't want to use tea leaves or bags, clean with 120 ml of white vinegar per bucket of water. If the wood is unsealed, sprinkle bicarb then splash white vinegar over the top. Scrub, then rinse with water.

To clean old urine stains on wood, use sugar soap. You may also need to repaint the wood or top up the varnish.

Problem:	**Squeaky floorboards.**
What to use:	**Talcum powder, wax.**
How to apply:	The squeakiness is usually caused by the boards rubbing together. Dust the floor with talcum powder, which will work its way between the boards and create a barrier. Then wax normally. I discovered this living in a house where all the floorboards were squeaky except the ones in the bathroom where talcum powder was scattered. I scattered talcum powder in the other rooms and they stopped squeaking. Great discovery!

Q: 'I've got double-sided carpet tape on my floor-boards,' says Diana. 'When I try to remove it, it lifts the varnish as well. What can I do?'

Problem:	**Adhesive on wood.**
What to use:	**Sticky tape, cloth, hot water, cling film, tea tree oil, tissues.**
How to apply:	Remove as much of the adhesive gum as possible by putting sticky tape over the top and quickly lifting it. Do this several times. Then dampen a cloth in hot water and lay it on top of the tape. Place cling film over the top of the cloth and leave for 5 minutes. Remove the cling film and the cloth and apply tea tree oil over the adhesive gum. Then roll the adhesive gum off with tissues.

Tiles

One house I lived in had Spanish tiles with dark-coloured cement grout. Every time I cleaned, the edge of the tiles used to smear with dirt. That's because the previous owners never cleaned the grout and it had collected layers of dirt and grime. I recommend using a plastic scourer (not a steel one) for this task. Simply stand on it and rub the scourer backwards and forwards over the grout.

To clean tiles, sprinkle with bicarb then splash white vinegar and mop the floor. Then rinse with hot water. The white vinegar may cause the room to smell a bit like a salad but this will dissipate and has the added benefit of making the floor non-slip. To seal terracotta tiles or unglazed Spanish quarry tiles, mix 1 part Unibond PVA to 20 parts water, mop it over the surface and leave it to dry completely – between one and four hours, depending on the weather. The seal will last for about three months.

: 'I've got a mop with a metal head and it's darkened my tiles,' reports Bill. 'Is there a solution?'

Problem:	Metal residue on tiles.
What to use:	Bicarb, white vinegar, nylon brush, hot water, sticky tape.
How to apply:	Sprinkle bicarb over the tiles, then splash with white vinegar and rub with a nylon brush. Rinse with hot water. To prevent the problem, put sticky tape over the metal.

Concrete

 Kerry's family had big plans to build their dream
home. 'We bought a block of land in a valley and
built a makeshift shed to live in while we
constructed the main house. Time went by and we
didn't end up building the house but decided to
stay in the shed and do it up instead. But we've
been living in it for eleven years and the concrete
floor slab has become really dirty. How can we
clean the slab before we put some tiles down?'

Problem:	**Dirty concrete floor.**
What to use:	**Bicarb, white vinegar, stiff brush or stiff broom, mop.**
How to apply:	Sprinkle bicarb over the surface, splash white vinegar over the bicarb, then scrub with a stiff brush or stiff broom. Rinse with warm water and a mop. If it's really dirty you may need to do this a few times.

Carpet

Buy the best quality carpet you can afford because the better the
quality, the less wear and tear you'll get. One of my sisters bought
cheap carpet and she had to replace it after five years. It's just not
worth it. Vacuum once a week, although this will vary depending
on the amount of traffic and dirt the carpet gets. I'd suggest using a
carpet cleaner every three months. After spraying the foam over the
carpet, scrub it with a broom head wrapped in an old clean white
T-shirt. Leave it to dry for about an hour, then vacuum. Doing this
fairly regularly means your carpet never gets dirty enough to need a
steam clean.

I like to clean woven carpet by scattering unprocessed wheat bran across the top of it and scrubbing with a dry broom. Then vacuum. If the carpet is particularly grimy, damp wheat bran with white vinegar to form a clumpy, but not wet, mix and scatter it over the carpet. Then scrub with a broom before vacuuming.

To freshen up dingy carpets, make up a spray bottle containing 1 part bicarb to 3 parts white vinegar and 5 parts water. Spray the carpet then sponge it, but don't go overboard and soak it. Sprinkling bicarb on the carpet before vacuuming is a good general carpet freshener, but won't necessarily clean stains. These will have to be spot cleaned.

Never put an iron on carpet. It will leave scorch marks on natural carpets and melt nylon or polyester ones.

CARPETS AND RUGS

Here's a tip from how to clean carpet from *Lee's Priceless Recipes*, 1817: If you have dark-coloured carpet, you can revive its colour. Grate two potatoes, cover them in hot water, leave for 2 hours then strain. Dip a brush into the liquid and wipe it over the carpet. The colour should brighten. Don't use this on light carpets.

If you have rugs, take them outside, hang them over the clothes line and whack them with a heavy item such as a tennis racquet, cricket bat or golf club, although be careful not to bend it! Vacuum the room.

Q: 'You've got to help me!' pleads Ali. 'I've got permanent marker on my brown nylon carpet and it looks awful.'

Problem: Permanent marker on carpet.

What to use: Egg white, brush.

How to apply: This is a difficult problem to fix. Try to remove the marker with egg white. Paint egg white over the permanent marker stain, leave it to dry then brush the egg white away with your fingers. The permanent marker should adhere to the egg white. Unfortunately, you will still have a slight shadow but the stain will be much improved.

> **HINT**
>
> **If you drop candle wax on carpet or fabric**
> Put ice on the wax to harden it then scrape as much away as possible with a blunt knife. Wedge a metal comb underneath the wax and put a paper towel on top of the wax, then use a hairdryer over it. The paper towel will absorb the wax. Repeat until all the wax is removed. Never use an iron on carpet as it can char natural fibres or melt synthetic fibres.

Q: 'We have an elderly dog,' says Annie, 'and he's losing it a little bit. The other day he did a big poop in the hallway and walked it up and down the wool Berber carpet. What can we do?'

Problem: Pet mishaps on carpet/fabric.

What to use: Paper towel, bicarb, white vinegar, sponge or nylon brush, vacuum cleaner/bucket, cold water, washing up liquid, old toothbrush, white vinegar, water, bicarb, vacuum cleaner/lavender oil, cotton wool ball, or camphor or mothballs; or

bicarb, sponge, white vinegar, nylon brush, vacuum cleaner or stiff brush/ultraviolet light, chalk.

How to apply: Remove as much of the solids as possible then blot with a paper towel until the carpet is touch dry. Sprinkle a little bicarb over the spot then splash a little white vinegar. Scrub with a sponge or nylon brush and leave to dry. Then vacuum it out and, if there's any scent, do it again. Another way to fix the problem is to fill a bucket with cold water and enough washing up liquid to generate a sudsy mix. Apply the detergent suds with an old toothbrush, using as little water as possible. Then fill a bucket with warm water and washing up liquid and apply the suds to the stain again with an old toothbrush. The reason you use both cold and warm water is because faeces contain proteins and fats. Leave to dry. Get rid of any pet urine smell by blotting with white vinegar and water. Then sprinkle with bicarb, allow it to dry and vacuum. Never soak urine stains on carpet because this will just push the stain further into the fibres.

Because animals like to return to the same spot, put a small amount of lavender oil on a cotton wool ball and lightly wipe it over the spot. This will deter dogs. Use a combination of camphor and water to deter cats unless you have coloured carpet, in which case put some mothballs near the spot as camphor can bleach carpet.

For old pet stains, cover the spot with a large amount of bicarb then wipe with a sponge dipped in white vinegar and scrub with a nylon brush. Dry thoroughly. Then vacuum or sweep with a stiff brush.

In the rather infuriating situation of being able to smell but not locate an old stain, use an ultraviolet (UV) light, not a black light. UV lights can be hired from a DIY shop. Under the light, the stains will fluoresce and glow. (Don't look into the ultraviolet light because it could damage your eyes and, unless you want a tan, don't stand in front of it.) Mark the stains with chalk. Then you've got the task of cleaning the stain up and a lot of bicarb and a little white vinegar will come to your aid. Because the stains have been there for a while, you may have to repeat the treatment a few times.

Problem:	**Fruit stain on carpet.**
What to use:	**White cloth, white vinegar, glycerine, cotton wool or old toothbrush, talcum powder, vacuum cleaner, carpet cleaner or Vanish Oxi Action, paper towel.**
How to apply:	Make sure the carpet is colour-fast*. For stains from fruits that go brown such as apricots, kiwi fruit, apples, bananas and so on, put glycerine on the stain with a cotton wool ball or old toothbrush and sprinkle talcum powder over the top of it. Vacuum. Then use a carpet cleaner. Vacuum again. An alternative to carpet cleaner is a paste of water and Vanish Oxi Action on the stain for a few minutes. Wipe it off, rinse and dry with a paper towel, leave the carpet to dry, then vacuum.

* To test for colour-fastness, soak a white cloth in white vinegar and apply to part of the carpet not on display. If any colour comes off, it's not colour-fast and you may have to patch the carpet. How to do this is explained in 'How to patch carpet' later (see p. 163).

Q:

'The kids spilled orange juice all over the carpet,' says Tina. 'How can I get it out?'

Problem: **Orange juice stain on carpet.**

What to use: **Carpet cleaner, cloth, lemon juice, ultraviolet light, cardboard.**

How to apply: For fresh orange juice stains apply carpet cleaner. If the stain has set, wipe a cloth dipped in lemon juice over the stain before applying carpet cleaner. Then bleach it with sunlight. If you can't get the stain into the sun, hire an ultraviolet lamp. Protect the unstained part of the carpet with cardboard, cutting a hole around the stain. If you don't, the unstained carpet will bleach as well. Leave the lamp on the stain for up to 24 hours, checking every two hours. Don't look into the ultraviolet light because it could damage your eyes.

Q:

'I tried to get an orange juice spill out of the carpet with washing up liquid and warm water,' reports Lynn, 'and now the stain has set and gone rusty. I need help!'

Problem: **Orange juice stain set on carpet.**

What to use: **Vanish Oxi Action, cloths, paper towels.**

How to apply: Lynn's effort had the effect of setting the stain. Test in an unobtrusive spot to make sure this remedy won't leach the colour*. Unset the stain with a paste of water and Vanish Oxi Action, leaving it for a few minutes. Then remove the paste with a cloth and blot any moisture with a paper towel. You may have

to repeat this process a couple of times. Be careful
not to get water on the carpet base or it will stain.
Have lots of paper towels at hand to absorb any
moisture immediately. Repeat if necessary.

* If the carpet isn't colour-fast (check by soaking a white cloth in
white vinegar and applying to a part of the carpet not on display; if
any colour comes off, it's not colour-fast), you may have to patch
the carpet. How to do this is explained later.

Q: 'One of the kids spilled lemonade on our dark-pink
carpet some time ago and we can't shift it,'
complains Michael. 'Do you have a suggestion?'

Problem: Old lemonade/sugar stain on carpet.

What to use: Glycerine, cotton wool ball, sponge or cloth,
bicarb, nylon brush, clean white cloth, white
vinegar/washing up liquid, water, nylon brush,
paper towel.

How to apply: A sugar stain is very difficult to remove because it
seeps right into the back of the carpet. For old stains,
apply some glycerine to the stain with a cotton wool
ball, and leave for a few minutes. Then wipe it off
with a sponge or cloth. Sprinkle bicarb over the stain
and scrub it in with a nylon brush. Then soak a clean
white cloth in white vinegar, wring it out and place it
over the bicarb. Stand on the cloth so it absorbs the
bicarb and stain. You may need to repeat this a few
times. If the stain still doesn't shift, mix washing up
liquid and water to create a sudsy mix and scrub the
suds into it with a nylon brush. Then place a paper
towel over the spot to absorb the stain. You may
need to repeat this a few times.

Q:

'Our house was broken into,' says Robyn. 'The police came and collected fingerprints, but they left all this black powder on the carpet and I don't know how to get it off. I rang the police and they didn't know either.'

Problem: **Black ink stain on carpet.**
What to use: **Milk, cloth, washing up liquid, lemon juice.**
How to apply: The black powder is ink-based. Rot some milk in the sun (the time it takes will vary) and rub the solids into the stain with a cloth. Leave for a few minutes then wash with a little washing up liquid, lemon juice and water.

Q:

'I'm in big trouble,' admits John. 'I dropped a full plate of spaghetti bolognese on beige carpet and a white cotton sofa. It's a part of the house where eating usually isn't permitted. Can I be redeemed?'

Problem: **Spaghetti bolognese stain on carpet/fabric.**
What to use: **Soap, sponge, ultraviolet light, cardboard.**
How to apply: Because spaghetti bolognese contains protein, use cold water and soap with a sponge to remove the proteins first. Then use an ultraviolet light. Cover the non-stained area with cardboard to protect it and leave the light on the stain for up to 24 hours, checking it every two hours. (Don't look into the ultraviolet light because it could damage your eyes.) You can do this with the sofa too, but putting it in the sun is better.

Q: 'I was enjoying a beer on a very hot day but spilled some on our white carpet,' says Ross. 'I did it yesterday and the added complication is it's dark beer. What should I do?'

Problem:	**Beer stain on carpet.**
What to use:	**White vinegar, paper towel, washing up liquid, cold water, old toothbrush.**
How to apply:	Because the stain is a day old, damp it with white vinegar and blot it with paper towel. You'll absorb even more of the stain if you roll the paper towel into a ball and stand on it. Then add washing up liquid to cold water to generate a sudsy mix and spread the suds over the stain with an old toothbrush. Use as little water as possible. Let it dry and repeat the process until it's clean. For a new stain, remove as much of the beer as possible with a paper towel then mix washing up liquid with cold water and apply the suds to the stain.

Problem:	**Blu-Tack stain on carpet.**
What to use:	**Ice, plastic bag, scissors, sticky tape, talcum powder, tea tree oil, cotton wool ball, tissue.**
How to apply:	Removing Blu-Tack from carpet is quite difficult. Place ice on the Blu-Tack first, either directly or inside a plastic bag. The Blu-Tack should become stiff and you can cut most of it off with scissors. Don't cut the carpet fibres. Put sticky tape over the Blu-Tack and rip it up several times. Then sprinkle talcum powder over the remaining Blu-Tack and roll it between your fingers. The powder will draw the

Blu-Tack out. For the remainder of the stain, use a little tea tree oil on a cotton wool ball and rub it in a circle. Then rub a tissue over it and the Blu-Tack should stick to the tissue.

Q: 'I had some friends over to watch a DVD and one of them dropped red wine on the carpet,' says Steven. 'What's the best way to get it out?'

Problem:	**New red-wine stain on carpet.**
What to use:	**Bicarb, vacuum cleaner, white vinegar, nylon brush.**
How to apply:	Cover the stain with a good amount of bicarb and let it dry for a few minutes. Then vacuum and re-apply a smaller amount of bicarb, add a little white vinegar and scrub with a nylon brush. Leave it to dry, then vacuum.

Problem:	**Old red-wine stain on carpet.**
What to use:	**Cloth, white vinegar.**
How to apply:	Damp the stain with a cloth dipped in white vinegar.

Problem:	**Boot polish stains and scuff marks on carpet.**
What to use:	**Eucalyptus oil, cotton wool.**
How to apply:	Rub eucalyptus oil over the spot with a cotton wool ball.

Problem:	**Fat-based food stain on carpet.**
What to use:	**Paper towel, hairdryer, bucket, washing up liquid, old toothbrush.**
How to apply:	Roll some paper towel into a ball, warm the carpet with a hairdryer then place the ball of paper towel over the stain. Stand on the paper towel so that as

much of the fat as possible is absorbed. Fill a bucket with warm water and enough washing up liquid to generate a sudsy mix. Apply the suds to the stain with an old toothbrush and scrub using as little water as possible. Place a clean paper towel over the stain and stand on it. Leave to dry.

Problem:	**Candle wax stain on carpet.**
What to use:	**Ice, blunt knife, metal comb, paper towel, hairdryer.**
How to apply:	Put ice on the wax to harden it then scrape as much away as possible with a blunt knife. Wedge a metal comb underneath the wax and put a paper towel on top of the wax. Then use a hairdryer over it. The paper towel will absorb the wax. Repeat until all the wax is removed. Never use an iron on carpet as it can char natural fibres or melt synthetic fibres.

Q: 'My two-year-old wanted to help me bring the shopping in,' reports Megan. 'So I gave her a carton of cream which she dropped on a green rug. It's created a white shadow and really smells. What can I do?'

Problem:	**Cream stain on rug/carpet.**
What to use:	**Detergent, old toothbrush, paper towel.**
How to apply:	Attack the proteins first. Mix enough washing up liquid in cold water to generate a sudsy mix and apply just the suds to the stain with an old tooth-brush. Then dry with paper towel. Remove the fats with detergent suds mixed in hot water. Apply the suds only to the stain with an old toothbrush, then dry with a paper towel.

Problem:	**Old coffee and tea stains on carpet.**
What to use:	**Glycerine, cotton wool ball, sponge, white vinegar, bicarb, vacuum cleaner.**
How to apply:	Apply glycerine to the stain with a cotton wool ball. Leave for 5 minutes then damp sponge the stain with white vinegar. Sprinkle with bicarb then vacuum when dry.

Q: 'What can you do about old vomit stains in the carpet?' asks Maryann.

Problem:	**Old vomit stains on carpet.**
What to use:	**Glycerine, cotton wool ball, milk, cloth, vacuum cleaner, cloth, carpet cleaner.**
How to apply:	How to clean vomit will depend on what's in it. Because the stain has been there for some time, apply glycerine with a cotton wool ball to the stain. Then rot some milk in the sun (the time it takes will vary) and apply the solids to the stain with a cloth. Leave until almost dry, vacuum and then wash the solids out with a damp cloth. Then clean the area with carpet cleaner.

Q: 'My wife opened a tube of foundation make-up and dropped it all over our white wool carpet,' reports Brian. 'Is there a way to get it out?'

Problem: Make-up on carpet.

What to use: Detergent, old toothbrush, paper towel, carpet cleaner/lemon juice or ultraviolet light, cardboard.

How to apply: Work out if the make-up has oil in it first. If it contains oil, clean that out by mixing washing up liquid in cold water and applying just the suds to the stain with an old toothbrush. Dry with a paper towel. Then clean the area with carpet cleaner. Sunlight will bleach the stain. If you can't get the carpet into the sun, apply some lemon juice to the stain or hire an ultraviolet light. Protect the unstained part of the carpet by covering it with cardboard or it will bleach as well. Leave the ultraviolet light on the stain for up to 24 hours, checking it every two hours. Don't look into the ultraviolet light because it could damage your eyes.

Problem: Singe/burn on carpet.

What to use: White cloth, white vinegar, 3 per cent hydrogen peroxide, damp cloth, scissors.

How to apply: Test the carpet for colour-fastness first. Do this by soaking a white cloth in white vinegar and applying it to a part of the carpet not on display. If any colour comes off, it's not colour-fast. If it is colour-fast, cut a cloth to the size of the burn and dip it in 3 per cent hydrogen peroxide. Then lay it over the mark for two minutes. Rinse with a damp cloth. If the burn is very bad or the carpet isn't colour-fast, clip the surface of the wool with scissors or patch it. How to do this is explained in How to patch carpet later (see p.163).

Q: 'I was cooking some chips in the oven and thought I'd been very clever putting some baking paper down first to collect the fat,' says Beverly. 'After we'd eaten, I bunched the baking paper up and transported it to the bin. But I obviously didn't close off all the corners because when I turned around, I discovered a trail of oil drips right across my carpet. I've tried to clean it with bicarb, commercial cleaners, a hot iron and dry-cleaning fluid. Nothing has worked!'

Problem:	Cooking fat on the carpet.
What to use:	Water, washing up liquid, toothbrush, paper towel or chamois sponge block.
How to apply:	Fill a bucket with cold water and enough washing up liquid to generate a sudsy mix. Then apply the suds to the stain and scrub with an old toothbrush. Use as little water as possible. Then dry the spot with a paper towel or a chamois sponge block. Allow it to dry out and repeat the process until the stain has cleared. Detergent helps break down fats and brings them to the surface.

Q: 'It's a rather sad story,' warns Bronwyn. 'My husband and I went away for the weekend and left the three teenage boys at home. The dog had an accident on the carpet and one of the boys cleaned it with the first thing he found in the cupboard, which was tile cleaner. He sprayed it on the carpet and now there's half an acre of brown on the carpet. What can I do?'

Problem: Tile cleaner sprayed on carpet.
What to do: Patch the carpet.

How to patch carpet

Cut around damaged part of the carpet into a manageable shape with a Stanley knife. Find a piece of the carpet (perhaps some leftover or cut from somewhere little seen, such as from inside a cupboard) a little larger than the stained area. Make sure the pattern is in the same direction. Then make a paper template of the stained area and transfer this to the piece of patch carpet. Cut the patch carpet around the template with a sharp knife. You'll need some carpet tape, which is available from carpet manufacturers, dealers and hardware shops. Attach the tape under the edges of the damaged carpet so that the adhesive side is facing upwards. Make sure that half of the tape is under the old carpet and the other half is exposed in the hole. Then press the patch carpet into the hole, sticking it to the exposed half of the tape. Brush the carpet in both directions until the fibres line up on the edges. Stand on the area for five minutes to make sure it sticks well. Then place a book on top of the patch for 24 hours.

Rugs and mats

Rugs are handy for high-traffic areas and if you have children. The less dirt a rug or mat accumulates, the longer it will last. And, unlike carpet, you can take it outside and give it a good whack.

To take care of an Oriental rug, give it a vacuum, then wrap a hair brush in an old T-shirt that's been soaked in a small amount of hair conditioner and warm water. Brush the rug with this until it's damp but not wet. This will keep the fibres soft. Once you've finished, use the hairbrush again, without the T-shirt, to fluff the fibres up. Then vacuum again. The number of times you'll need to do this will

depend on how much traffic the rug gets. If it has a lot of feet
tramping over it, do this every two months. Your rugs are less likely
to absorb stains if you Scotchgard them after cleaning.

Problem:	**Rug/mat edge is lifting.**
What to use:	**Rubber mesh or wire claw.**
How to apply:	One option is to place a rubber mesh on the back of the rug or mat. Another option is to attach a wire claw to the edge of the rug to help keep it flat. Both are available from carpet manufacturers.

Sisal

Sisal is best cleaned by sweeping. Never use wet cleaners on it. I
find the best cleaning method is mixing unprocessed wheat bran and
white vinegar until clumpy but not wet. Scatter it over the sisal and
sweep backwards and forwards, then vacuum. Wheat bran acts as
a scourer and absorbent.

Coir

This type of flooring attracts insects so vacuum regularly. To deter
insects, leave mint bags in the corner of the room. Use a mixture of
wheat bran and white vinegar to clean, as described with sisal.

Linoleum, vinyl and self-levelling plastics

Linoleum, or lino, is formed by coating hessian or canvas with
linseed oil. Developments with plastics mean there are now
numerous variations on the lino theme. Clean by sprinkling bicarb
over the surface, then splashing white vinegar on top and mopping.
Then rinse with hot water and leave to dry.

Q: 'I've got large marks from a ballpoint pen on my lino floor,' reports Julie. 'How do I get it off?'

Problem:	Ink/ballpoint pen stain on linoleum.
What to use:	Milk, old toothbrush.
How to apply:	Rot some milk in the sun. Scrub the solids into the stain with an old toothbrush, then wash out.

DOORS

One of my tricks if the house is a bit untidy and visitors are about to arrive is to wipe the door jambs with lavender oil. The smell creates an impression of cleanliness and also keeps insects away! Clean doors every couple of months or when they become grubby. If the door has a high polish or laminate finish, clean with washing up liquid and water. If it has a French polish finish, use a good quality, non-silicone furniture polish. Wipe greasy hand marks with a damp cloth. Door handles made of chrome, brass or glass should be cleaned with bicarb and white vinegar on one sponge.

If your door squeaks, rub the hinges with soap. If the door lock is jammed or stiff, use a graphite puffer either into the hole of the lock or in the slots around the edge of the lock tongue. If the door is sticking and you can't work out where to sand it, rub chalk down the doorframe, shut the door and the chalk will transfer to the part of the jamb that needs sanding.

LAMPS AND LIGHT SHADES

Lamps illuminate a room and are generally responsible for creating the mood as well. Light shades made of fabric should be dry cleaned or cleaned with carpet cleaner. Once the carpet cleaner has dried, use the brush head on your vacuum cleaner to remove it. Make sure the brush is clean first or you'll create more mess. Glass light shades should be cleaned in warm water. Clean brass and metal arms with a good quality brass polish. And make sure you don't get cleaning product in the electrical fittings. To cut down on insects, spray the tops of light shades with non-toxic surface insecticide spray.

Every time you change a light bulb, clean all other light bulbs with a cloth and they'll shine brighter. To prevent halogen lights corroding, wipe the connection on the bulb with a cloth once a week.

Problem:	**Broken light bulb in light socket.**
What to use:	**Rubber gloves, carrot.**
How to apply:	Make sure the light is off and that you're wearing some rubber gloves. Get a carrot, cut the top off and jam the carrot base into the light bulb socket. Then twist or turn and remove. Make sure you remove any small pieces of broken glass before putting in a new light bulb.

Cleaning chandeliers

They're beautiful and decadent and difficult to clean. However, the task of cleaning is made a little easier with the product Crystal Clear. Turn the light off at the switch and put a sheet or towel underneath the chandelier of a size suitable to cover the entire drip area. Using a ladder so you can reach the chandelier comfortably, remove the light bulbs and put a small plastic bag over each of the fittings so you don't get moisture in the electrics. Dust the tops of the chandelier with a soft brush then spray a generous amount of Crystal Clear until the chandelier is damp and starting to drip. The dirt and dust will run off. If it's been a while since you last cleaned it, you may need to apply Crystal Clear again. When the chandelier is completely dry, clean and return the light bulbs.

WALLS

It's inevitable that you'll get marks on the walls, especially in high-traffic areas or if you have little people with grubby hands who use the wall as a convenient support. Be careful using commercial products to clean marks because most have an alcohol base that can break down the paint surface and leave a bleached shiny spot.

Walls, skirting boards, cornices and the ceiling should be dusted regularly. If they're very dirty, dampen an old T-shirt in white vinegar and water, then wrap the T-shirt around a broom head, fix it with elastic bands and wipe it over the walls. Pay particular attention to the area above the stove.

Clean your walls every couple of weeks either with a broom or vacuum cleaner. Put an old T-shirt over the top of the broom or vacuum to prevent bristle marks. Some dirty marks will come off with a good pencil eraser. You could also try rolling brown bread into a ball and rubbing it against the wall. If these don't work, try a very diluted solution of sugar soap applied with a soft cloth. Wring the cloth tightly before applying. For build-up around switches, apply white vinegar and water sparingly with a sponge. To avoid drip lines, start cleaning from the bottom and work your way up, drying as you go. To prevent spider webs on the ceiling and wall edges, put a small drop of lemon oil on your cobweb brush. Spiders don't like lemons.

Problem:	**Mould on the wall.**
What to use:	**Oil of cloves, bucket, soft cloth or sponge.**
How to apply:	Put 4–5 drops of oil of cloves in a bucket half filled with water. Wipe this over the mouldy wall with a soft cloth or sponge. The mould may not come off all at once but the oil of cloves will continue to kill it. Dust the mould off later.

Problem: **Double-sided tape on the wall.**
What to use: **Detergent, clean fabric, cling film.**
How to apply: Add a little washing up liquid to boiling water, wet some clean fabric in it, wring it out and place it over the tape. Then put cling film over the top of the fabric and leave until the heat penetrates the glue. You should be able to lift the edge of the tape with your fingers when it's ready. Never use a knife because you can tear the paint on the wall.

DID YOU KNOW? To remove spider webs, attach an old T-shirt or rag to the wand of your vacuum tube and secure it with an elastic band. Then vacuum the spider webs. Using the rag means the sticky webs will land there rather than get stuck inside the vacuum tube.

HINT

How to remove a spider without using insecticide
Find an old ice-cream or takeaway container with a lid. Put the container over the top of the spider then slide the lid underneath so you capture the spider. Then either take the spider outside or flush it down the toilet. If the spider is out of reach, use the bristles of a broom to reach the spider. If the spider's eyes are facing the bristles, it will climb onto them. If not, it will run away. Allow the spider to climb onto the bristles, then bring the broom down to the floor and put the container over the top of the spider. Slide the lid underneath so that the spider is contained. Release the spider outside or flush it down the toilet.

Wallpaper

A slice of fresh bread rubbed over wallpaper is a great way to clean it. The kind of bread you use should depend on the colour of the wallpaper. Brown bread is more abrasive but may transfer colour to light walls.

 Q: 'I've got three boys under the age of ten and, one day, they decided to plaster the wallpaper with peanut butter, jam and margarine,' says Jane. 'It's a disaster!'

Problem:	**Peanut butter, jam, margarine on wallpaper.**
What to use:	**Detergent, paper towel, damp cloth.**
How to apply:	Do not use water. Put washing up liquid onto a paper towel and wipe it over the wallpaper. The washing up liquid will break down the fats in the food. You'll need to do this several times. Then wipe with a damp cloth.

PICTURES, PAINTINGS AND MIRRORS

Look after your paintings just in case the one you inherited from Uncle Harry is worth a fortune. Even if you don't have a hidden treasure, care should still be taken looking after them.

Acrylic paintings can be cleaned with a damp cloth.

To remove residue and dust from oil paintings, clean with stale urine, salt and potato. Yes, you did read stale urine! Collect 1 litre of female urine and leave it in the sun for a week. It will reduce to ½ litre. Then add 1 tablespoon of salt and 2 tablespoons of raw grated potato to it. Allow the mixture to sit for half an hour. Dampen a cloth in the mixture, wring it and then wipe over the painting. Then damp a clean cloth in water and wipe the painting gently. Pat it dry. You can also rub brown bread over the painting to clean it. For any serious cleaning problems, see a restorer.

Water colours should be cleaned by a professional.

Most gilding is covered with a layer of shellac and alcohol-based cleaners will compromise it. Instead, dust the frame with a hairdryer on the cool setting. This should be enough to clean it, but if dirt remains, wipe a damp cloth over the frame and then dry it with a soft cloth.

Polycarbonate should only be cleaned with a damp cloth. Clean metal and wood as you would furniture. Clean plastic with glycerine.

Protect paintings by spraying a cloth with non-toxic surface insecticide spray and wiping it over the back of picture frames. Don't touch the painting, just the frames.

Rather than buying a new mirror, which can be very expensive, find a lovely old second-hand frame and see a glazier who will supply, cut and fit a mirror to size very cheaply.

Problem:	**Flaked or chipped gilding.**
What to use:	**Soft cloth, Gilder's Size and Gilder's Gold Dust.**
How to apply:	Clear any dust with a soft cloth then paint the bare section with a thin coat of Gilder's Size. Allow it to dry until it's tacky then dust with Gilder's Gold Dust, which is very fine gold dust. Brush off any excess.

WINDOWS

When cleaning windows, always use vertical stripes on the outside and horizontal stripes on the inside. That way you can tell which side a smudge is on. The vertical stripes should be on the outside because that's the way rain falls, and any horizontal lines catch moisture and dust and leave grimy lines. Vertical lines allow the dirt to run away, leaving windows looking cleaner for longer. Don't use newspaper to clean windows. They used to be good when the ink contained lamp black, but today's newspapers use rubber-based ink, which leaves a smear. Use paper towels instead.

Window frames and sills

Every time you vacuum the floor, vacuum the windowsills as well. Then wipe them with a mixture of 240 ml of white vinegar to 1 bucket of water. Keep putty in good condition by wiping a small amount of linseed oil over it twice a year if the putty is unpainted. If the putty is painted, make sure it's painted all the way to the glass otherwise the putty will allow oil to smear out over the glass. To help prevent rubber seals perishing, wipe them with white vinegar and water. Never poke at silicone because if you break the seal it becomes exposed and mildew can grow. Clean it with water.

Clean marble windowsills with bicarb and 1 part white vinegar to 5 parts water. Then polish with cera wax. To inhibit mildew, add 1 drop of oil of cloves to half a cup of cera wax.

For sandstone windowsills, clean with bicarb and white vinegar. Inhibit mildew by adding oil of cloves to hot rinse water.

Clean painted wooden windowsills with white vinegar and water. If they're varnished, clean with a good quality, non-silicone furniture polish. Wipe unsealed cedar with a good quality furniture oil that will continue to feed the wood. If it's gone grey, wipe it with a wet tea bag, then allow it to dry before oiling it.

Rubbing a cake of soap along the window frame and sashes will allow the window to move more smoothly.

> **HINT**
>
> There is a knack to cleaning window sills. Use the fine nozzle or brush head on the vacuum cleaner and vacuum all the dust. Wipe over with a cloth that's been wrung out in water. If there's any build-up of grime in the corners, wrap a cloth that's been wrung out in water over a butter knife and reach into the corners. You can clean sashes in the same way. The window action will work better if it's kept clean.

Curtains

Someone living on a busy road will have to clean their curtains more often than someone living in a sleepy hollow. Hand wash or, if necessary, dry clean curtains (it's best if you can ensure this is non-toxic) according to the instructions. After washing coloured curtains, hang them upside down so the colour doesn't run. Don't dry them in direct sunlight or they'll bleach.

To clean chintz and cretonne curtains, place 115 g of unprocessed wheat bran in a saucepan with 1 litre of water and slowly bring it to the boil. Let it simmer for a few minutes and then strain it. Combine the strained liquid with an equal amount of lukewarm water. Dip the curtains and then hang them straight. This will clean and stiffen the fabric. If you need to replace the sheen on chintz or cretonne, use a combination of 1 part glycerine, 1 part egg white and 20 parts water in a spray pack. Spray it on the front surface of the fabric then use a warm iron. Don't use this on muslin, net or fine lace.

Velvet curtains should be cleaned with wheat bran in either a muslin or silk bag. Rub the bag over the tufts.

When ironing curtains, always iron top to bottom. This will keep the top edges straight and the curtains will hang better. If you don't want to iron the curtains rehang them slightly damp and allow them to dry in fresh air. Just make sure the windows are clean or you'll have dirty curtains again.

Q: *'My cat sprayed on my new curtains,' says Chris. 'The smell is awful and there's a slight stain.'*

Problem: Cat spray on curtains.
What to use: Vanish, lavender oil, spray pack, camphor flakes.

How to apply: To remove the stain, wash the curtains in a bucket
with Vanish (for quantity, follow directions) and
water. Add a few drops of lavender oil to the water
to get rid of the smell. Rinse and hang on the line. If
the smell remains, add a couple of drops of lavender
oil to water in a spray pack and spray over the area.
Leave some camphor flakes nearby to deter the cat.

Venetian blinds

Don't throw your old kitchen tongs out. They can be recycled and
reinvented as venetian blind cleaners. Glue some sponge to both
inside edges of the tongs and leave to set. Then place the tongs
over the top and bottom of each blind, pinch the tongs together and
run them along. The sponge can be wet or dry. To clean the cords,
use a mixture of white vinegar and water and apply with a sponge.
Start from the top and wipe down so the liquid soaks into the cord.
The second time you do this, squeeze the moisture from the cord.
You may have to do this a few times to remove all the dirt.

To clean venetian blinds thoroughly, take them down and lay
them outside. Fill a bucket with a mild detergent solution and then,
with a broom, wash the venetians backwards and forwards, shutting
one side and then the other. Hang them on the clothes line and
wash them down with a hose. Leave to dry.

Wooden blinds and plantation shutters

Wooden blinds and shutters can be dusted in the same way as
venetian blinds – with those old tongs! You can also clean them by
putting on some white gloves and running your fingers along the
top and bottom of the slats. The only problem is your fingers may
become sore if there are a lot of blinds to clean.

Roman blinds

The hoisting mechanism of Roman blinds is complicated and delicate so have them cleaned professionally.

Q: 'I had a bee swarm in my house,' reports Sally. 'The bees dumped their nectar load all over the Roman blinds. Can I clean them?'

Problem:	**Bee nectar on blinds.**
What to use:	**Vanish Oxi Action, plate, cloth.**
How to apply:	Mix Vanish Oxi Action with water on a plate, dampen a cloth in it, wring it out and spot-clean the nectar spots. Leave to dry.

Problem:	**Insect droppings on blinds.**
What to use:	**Bucket, washing up liquid, cloth.**
How to apply:	Fill a bucket with water and enough washing up liquid to generate a sudsy mix. Apply the suds to the stains with a damp cloth.

Problem:	**Food splattered on blinds.**
What to use:	**Bucket, washing up liquid, cloth.**
How to apply:	Fill a bucket with water and enough washing up liquid to generate a sudsy mix. Apply the suds to the stains with a damp cloth.

CEILING

I moved into a house where the ceiling was drooping so much it looked like clouds. It had got that way because a couple of the tiles were loose and water had penetrated. But it was such a beautiful ceiling that I decided to salvage it. After asking around, I learned that hessian bags could do the trick. First, use a ceiling jack to lift and flatten the ceiling. Then soak the bags in resin. Climb into the ceiling cavity and place the bags over the wooden beams so that half the bag is resting on one side of the plaster and the other half on the other side. The resin in the hessian sticks to the ceiling plaster and, when it dries, draws up the plaster and stays hard. This is much cheaper than putting in a new ceiling!

Q: 'I can't stand the smell of naphthalene flakes,' reports Rebecca. 'I've put the flakes around to deter a rat at my place. Is there any way to get rid of the smell?'

Problem:	**Smell of naphthalene flakes.**
What to use:	**Lemon thyme.**
How to apply:	Sprinkle some lemon thyme wherever the naphthalene was placed. The better way to deter rats is with with snake poo, as explained below!

HINT

Getting rid of mice
When I lived in the Australian countryside, some mice took up residence in my house. After a while, I noticed they'd disappeared. A few months later, I saw a massive snake sliding from the ceiling, thankfully outside the house. Its length was the height of the building. Then the mice came back. I mentioned this to a neighbour who told me snakes deter mice. So the solution for mice is either to have a snake in the house or, more pleasantly, scatter some snake poo inside the ceiling or under the house. The poo is a small pellet, doesn't smell and should last for about twelve months. Ask your local pet shop for some.

CHAPTER 7:
The Bedrooms

We spend a third of our lives in the bedroom. Sure, most of it is spent sleeping, but when you're awake, it's your room. It's a sanctuary. How can you make your bed a joy to slumber in? And what can you do if breakfast in bed becomes breakfast all over the bed? Read on and all will be revealed. The bedroom is also where we keep our clothes. Care for them now and you'll still be able to wear them years later when they come back into fashion.

It's very easy for the bedroom to become a clutter zone. Maybe it's because clothes are put on and taken off here, contents of pockets are removed here, make-up is put on here and jewellery is stored here. There are lots of bits and pieces. It's why the rule of 'a place for everything' is paramount. Jennifer's father delights in telling the story of when she was about three years old, he'd come home from a long day at the office, collapsed into a chair and taken his shoes off. She firmly pronounced that 'your shoes should be either on your feet or in the cupboard, not on the floor'!

ASSEMBLE THE CLEAN KIT

beeswax – to polish
broom – to clean floors and walls
clothes basket – to transport dirty clothes to the laundry
clutter bucket – to transport displaced items
damp cloth – to wipe over surfaces
detergent (washing up liquid) – cleaning agent
dry cloth – to wipe over surfaces
elastic bands – to secure old T-shirts to broom heads
furniture polish cloth – to wipe over wooden furniture
lavender oil – fragrance
lemon peel – to apply beeswax and deter spiders
old T-shirt – to use as a cleaning cloth
paper towel – to wipe over surfaces

rags – to use as cleaning cloths
spray bottle – to hold either white vinegar or water
vacuum cleaner – to vacuum floors and window sills

CLEANING SPECIFIC TO THE BEDROOM

With your clutter bucket, clear anything from the room that doesn't belong there. Then strip the sheets from the bed, collect dirty clothes and leave them in a basket outside the door of the bedroom – you'll sort them later in the laundry. Dust the ceiling and light fittings with a soft broom or long-handled duster, then dust the walls and paintings, especially along the tops of frames or wall art. Wipe light switches and power points with white vinegar on a cloth. Wipe door jambs with either white vinegar or washing up liquid and water on a cloth adding lavender oil for fragrance. Don't forget windowsills because these are a dust-collecting zone. If a windowsill is really grimy, use a small amount of washing up liquid on a damp cloth.

Remove items, such as the clock radio, tissue boxes and lamps, from bedside tables and chests of drawers. Wipe all surfaces with a cloth tightly wrung out in water, working from the top of the room down. I prefer this to dusting with a dry cloth because it cleans better and traps the dust rather than fluffing it around the room.

Polish furniture according to the type of finish it has. For wooden surfaces, use a good non-silicone furniture polish with a drop of lavender oil for scent. For laminate finishes, just use a cloth tightly wrung out in water. Then replace items, cleaning them with a damp cloth as you return them.

Empty out the clutter bucket and take the washing to the washing machine. Add fragrance if you like. I mix my own using 2 drops of washing up liquid and 5 drops of lavender oil in a spray bottle of water. You can also use tea tree oil or any of the floral essential oils.

You'll save on cleaning time if the bedroom is arranged to maximise airflow. To achieve this, put the bed either between the window and door or between two windows. This allows air to flow across the bed and stops mould growing and that dank, mildewy smell. It helps keep the air dry. Dust sticks to damp surfaces more easily than dry ones. If you have room under your bed, use it for storage. To cut back on cleaning, use storage containers with lids to prevent dust getting in under the bed. It means less vacuuming.

BEDS

The importance of a clean and comfortable mattress becomes really evident when you don't have one. Just ask any backpacker, especially one scratching bedbug bites! I like to air, turn and vacuum mattresses often. If you can, let yours air for about 15 minutes every day before making the bed. And get into the habit of turning the mattress over and backwards, each week if possible. This may sound excessive but it keeps the coils even and stops the mattress from sagging. To help you remember where you are in the rotation cycle, attach a different coloured safety pin to each corner. I'd also recommend a monthly sprinkle of bicarb over the mattress; leave it for a couple of hours and then vacuum it off.

An indispensable part of any bedding is a mattress protector. It's a great washable barrier between you and the mattress and allows air to circulate. Wash it according to the instructions every third time you change your sheets. If you have a headboard, vacuum it once a week.

If you spill something on the mattress, use as little moisture as possible to clear it off. It's better to apply a few times than use too much at one time. Use a hairdryer to speed up the drying time.

How to kill dust mites and bedbugs

I suffer from asthma and use this remedy to kill dust mites. Put a tea bag into a spray bottle filled with cold water; let it sit for 3 minutes and then lightly spray the liquid over the mattress. The tannins in the tea kill mites.

And no matter how clean you are, you can get bedbugs, which live wherever people do. Bed bugs are about 3 mm long and look like flat leaves. Keep them contained with tea tree oil. Rub some onto your fingers and then wipe around the edge of the mattress, as well as along all the skirting boards and window frames. Use non-toxic surface insecticide spray over the edges and ends of the bed, but not over the top of the mattress and not just before you're about to sleep in the bed.

Wash all your bedding and dry it in the sun. The sun is a great antibacterial, antifungal and insecticide. You can also have a mattress commercially sanitised and debugged if needed. The procedure I've heard about uses a tea and UV formula. To stop the bites, rub lavender oil over your entire body before going to bed.

Problem:	**Tea stain on mattress.**
What to use:	**Glycerine, cotton wool, washing up liquid, cloth, hairdryer.**
How to apply:	Apply glycerine with a cotton wool ball. Use enough to make the surface of the mattress damp but not soaked. Leave for 10–15 minutes then wash it off with a little washing up liquid on a damp cloth. Leave to dry or speed dry with a hairdryer. Never hand a sleepy person a cup of tea in bed because it's likely to end up all over the mattress. It's happened to me!

Problem: **Coffee stain on mattress.**
What to use: **Glycerine, cotton wool, washing up liquid, cloth, hairdryer.**
How to apply: Apply glycerine with a cotton wool ball. Use enough to make the surface of the mattress damp but not soaked. Leave for 10–15 minutes then wash it off with a little washing up liquid on a damp cloth. Leave to dry or speed dry with a hairdryer.

Problem: **Fresh bloodstain on mattress.**
What to use: **Bar of soap, cloth.**
How to apply: Moisten the bar of soap with cold water and rub it on the stain, working from the outside to the inside of the stain. Rinse several times with a cloth wrung out in cold water. Leave it to dry and repeat if needed.

Problem: **Old bloodstain on mattress.**
What to use: **Cornflour, cloth, stiff brush.**
How to apply: Make a paste of cornflour and water to the consistency of thickened cream. Paint it on the stain with a cloth and leave to dry. Brush the dried mixture off with a stiff brush. You may need to do this a few times.

Q: 'I write a lot in bed,' says David. 'But I had a disaster when my ballpoint pen broke and ink went everywhere, including into the mattress. What should I do?'

Problem:	**Ink/ballpoint pen stain on the mattress.**
What to use:	**Milk, washing up liquid, cloth.**
How to apply:	Rot some milk in the sun (the time it takes will vary). Then place the milk solids on the stain, and with your hand, gently rub the solids in a circle over the stain. As the area dries, you will see the ink start to rise up through the milk solids. Remove the solids with some detergent suds on a cloth, using as little water as possible. If any odour remains, dampen the area with a cloth, cover with talcum powder and allow the powder to absorb the last of the odour.

Problem:	**Semen stain on the mattress.**
What to use:	**Bar of soap, cloth, ice.**
How to apply:	Dampen a bar of soap with cold water and rub it over the stain. Leave it for 2 minutes then rub the soap off with a damp cloth. Allow to dry. For old semen stains, ice the stain before applying soap.

Q: 'My child is a bed-wetter,' reports Jane. 'Urine has soaked into his mattress. What do you suggest?'

Problem:	**Urine stain on mattress.**
What to use:	**Detergent, cloth, hairdryer, lemon juice or white vinegar, cloth.**
How to apply:	Add a little washing up liquid to water to generate a sudsy mix. Scrub the suds into the stain with a cloth and, if you can, put the mattress in the sun. If you can't, use paper towels to dry as much as you can. Then dry with a hairdryer. Neutralise the smell with lemon juice or white vinegar applied sparingly with a damp cloth.

Problem:	**New red-wine stain on mattress.**
What to use:	**Old toothbrush, white vinegar, paper towel.**
How to apply:	Dip an old toothbrush in white vinegar and rub it over the stain. Blot the stain with paper towels. Repeat until clean. Dry thoroughly.

Problem:	**Old red-wine stain on mattress.**
What to use:	**Glycerine, cotton wool ball, bicarb, white vinegar, soft brush, washing up liquid, soapy sponge, paper towel, hairdryer, vacuum cleaner.**
How to apply:	Loosen the stain with glycerine applied with a cotton wool ball until the edge of the stain begins to lighten. Make a paste with 1 dessertspoon of bicarb and 2 dessertspoons of white vinegar and scrub into the stain. Wait until it stops fizzing, then rub it off with a soft brush. Leave until the stain begins to disappear. Then wipe it off with a damp soapy sponge. Blot with paper towels and dry with a hairdryer. Then vacuum.

Q: 'We've stored an inner-spring mattress in a caravan for six months,' reports Jenny. 'It really smells. What do you suggest?'

Problem:	**Smelly mattress.**
What to use:	**Household steamer, lavender oil, bicarb, vacuum cleaner.**
How to apply:	Hire a household steamer, put a couple of drops of lavender oil in the water and apply the steam to the entire mattress. A steamer works a bit like a reverse vacuum cleaner. Then put the mattress in the sunshine. If you can, lie it on top of the clothes line

so air can circulate around the mattress. If you can't get it into the sun, dust bicarb over the mattress and leave it until it's completely dry, then vacuum. Turn and repeat on the other side. Push up and down on the mattress while sniffing the air vents on the side of the mattress. If smell is released, you need to steam again!

HINT

If your mattress is damp, speed up the drying process with a hairdryer.

Pillows

I like my pillows in all shapes, sizes and densities. Pillows can be made of foam, feather, polyester or kapok. Use a pillow protector as well as a pillowcase and wash them weekly. The reason why you should use a protector is to stop the pillow compacting or needing as much washing. Wash pillows in woolwash the same way that you would wash your duvet as described on p.189. Allow them to dry in an elevated area so the water can drip away. The top of the clothes line is ideal. Turn the pillow regularly while it's drying but never compress it while it's wet. When you think it's dry, leave it for another hour to make sure the centre of it has dried completely.

Pillow protectors are quilt-like covers that equalise the pressure of your head on the pillow and help keep the pillow aerated. They allow more air to flow so your head sweats less and produces less oil, so you're less likely to get acne because everything stays cleaner. They'll even keep you warmer in winter, acting like a Thermos. The same applies with mattress protectors. More air is able to flow, so there's less sweat. If you can't afford a mattress protector or don't

like them, use a pure woollen blanket that can be bought very
cheaply and already sanitised from charity shops.

Sheets

There's nothing better than getting into bed with clean, fresh
sheets. When selecting sheets, choose natural fibres such as cotton,
silk or linen. I hate polyester satin sheets. They may look good but
they're cold in winter and like lying on a plastic bag in summer!
Wash your sheets once a week in a good detergent. If you can, dry
them in the sun because it's a great antibacterial and leaves them
smelling fresh. I love sheets to have that starchy feel. You can make
your own starch from rice. Strain the water after you cook rice and
then mix 240 ml of the rice-water starch with 240 ml plain water.
Add 120 ml of this mixture to the rinse cycle of the washing
machine. The sheets will be really white and firm against your skin
and the rice powder helps prevent sweat. Don't use rice-water
starch on satin sheets because it will affect their texture and
smoothness.

Cotton sheets can be washed with washing powder or liquid in
hot water. If they have blood or other protein stains, remove the
stain with cold water and soap before you wash. Polyester/cotton-
blend sheets can also be washed with washing powder or liquid in
hot water. If they have blood or other protein stains, remove with
cold water and soap before you wash. Flannelette sheets can be
washed with washing powder or liquid in hot water. If they have
blood or other protein stains, remove with cold water and soap
before you wash. Egyptian cotton sheets have a larger thread count
so the weave is stronger, finer and smoother. Wash them with
washing powder or liquid in hot water. If they have blood or other
protein stains, remove stains with cold water and soap before you
wash. Linen sheets should be washed with washing powder or liquid

in hot water. Satin sheets should be washed in cool water. Hang the sheets over the clothes line so the satin sides rest against each other. Remove the sheets from the line before they're completely dry and partially fold them. That way you won't have to iron them. Wash silk sheets with shampoo in blood-heat water and add a little hair conditioner to blood-heat rinse water.

With other accidental spills, work out what the stain is made of and then work out its solvent, remembering that protein stains need to be removed first with cold water before fat stains are removed with hot water. If you do it the other way around, you'll set the protein stain.

Problem:	**Tea stain on sheets.**
What to use:	**Glycerine, cotton wool balls.**
How to apply:	For fresh stains, rub glycerine into the stain with a cotton wool ball. Then put the sheets through the washing machine on the cold cycle.

Problem:	**Fruit juice stains on sheets.**
What to use:	**Vanish.**
How to apply:	Wash the sheets in the washing machine and hang them in sunshine. If you can't dry the sheets in the sun, soak them in Vanish before washing then tumble dry. If the sheets are white, use Vanish Oxi Action Crystal White. If the sheets are coloured, use Vanish Oxi Action.

Q: 'I had a cut on my knee which bled through the bandage and onto my sheets,' reveals Jessica. 'I washed the sheets in hot water, which has set the stain. Can it be fixed?'

Problem:	**Bloodstain on sheets.**
What to use:	**Bar of soap/Vanish/glycerine, cotton wool.**
How to apply:	Dampen the soap in cold water and rub over the stain. Then rub the stain against itself vigorously until it's removed. You may need to do this a few times. Put the sheets through the washing machine on the cold cycle. An alternative is to soak the stain in Vanish. If the stain has set, apply glycerine to either side of the stain with cotton wool. Rub in circles from the outside to the inside of the stain until it starts to shift at the edge, then wash in Vanish and cold water.

Problem:	**Semen stain on sheets.**
What to use:	**Bar of soap.**
How to apply:	Dampen the soap in cold water and rub over the stain. Then rub the stain against itself until it's removed. Wash the sheets on a cold cycle.

Problem:	**Egg yolk stain on sheets.**
What to use:	**Bar of soap, cold water, warm wash.**
How to apply:	Dampen the soap in cold water and rub over the stain. Then put the sheets through the washing machine on a warm setting to remove the fats.

Problem:	**Chocolate stain on sheets (not polyester satin).**
What to use:	**Bar of soap.**
How to apply:	Dampen the soap in cold water, then rub over the stain before soaking in cold water. Wash the sheets in the washing machine on a warm or hot cycle.

Problem: **Ink/ballpoint pen stain on sheets.**
What to use: **Milk.**
How to apply: Rot a carton of milk in the sun (the time this takes
will vary). Then heap the solids over the stain with
your hand. Leave until the ink starts to soak into the
solids. Then wash the rotten milk out in the washing
machine on the warm cycle.

Problem: **Vomit stain on sheets.**
What to use: **Vanish.**
How to apply: Rinse out the solids first with water, then put the
sheets through the washing machine and dry them
in the sun. If you can't dry them in the sun, soak
them in Vanish before putting them through the
washing machine. Then put them in the dryer.
Always wash vomit as soon as possible because
mould can grow on it overnight and will stain.

HINT

Common spills on sheets

Blood
Dampen some soap in cold water and rub over the
stain. Rub the stain against itself vigorously until it's
removed. You may need to do this a few times. Put the
sheets through the washing machine on the cold cycle.
An alternative is to soak the stained item in Vanish. If the
stain has set, apply glycerine with a cotton wool ball to
either side of the stain, rub in circles from the outside to
the inside of the stain until it starts to shift at the edge
then wash in Vanish and cold water.

Chocolate
Because chocolate contains protein, you must use cold
water. Dampen some soap in cold water, rub over the
stain then soak the sheets in cold water. Wash the sheets
in the washing machine on a warm or hot cycle.

Common spills on sheets

Coffee

For a new stain, use soap and cold water and rub the stain vigorously, then wash normally. For an old stain, apply glycerine and leave for 10–15 minutes, then put the sheets through the washing machine.

Vomit

Rinse the sheet with water and put it through the washing machine. If the staining is particularly bad, soak in Vanish first then put through the washing machine.

Duvets

Duvets can be made of goose feathers, wool or synthetics. Wash them twice a year or even more if you sweat a lot. You can tell it's time for a wash when the fibres are packed down and lumpy, or the duvet smells. Some duvets can be put through the washing machine. Just check the manufacturer's instructions first. Others, regardless of the filling, can be washed in a bath or large washing sink. If you don't have one, try to borrow a friend's.

Fill the bath with water warmed to blood temperature and half a cap of woolwash, or shampoo for a double-sized duvet. Lay the duvet in the bath then get in yourself and stomp up and down on the duvet until you get rid of all the dirt and grime. Empty the bath, fill it again with clean, blood-heat water and stomp over it again. Let the water out, fill the bath again with clean, blood-heat water and allow it to soak through the duvet.

After you've rinsed the duvet, drain the water from the bath and tread on the duvet to squeeze out as much moisture as possible. Place the duvet in a large black bin bag rather than a basket so you don't leave a drip trail. Then take the duvet outside and put it on an old sheet. If you don't have a lawn, place it flat over the top of the clothes line. Leave it to dry for quite some time, then shake it and turn it. You need to do this about three times until it's almost dry. Then hang it on the clothes line using lots of pegs so you don't put stress on any one spot. Unless you already have a stitched ridge, don't fold the duvet over the line. Instead, peg it by the two outside edges on separate lines so that it forms a U-shape. This allows air to circulate. When it's almost completely dry, whack it with your hand or an old tennis racquet. This fluffs up the fibres or loosens the feathers. Then put it back inside the duvet cover to protect it against spills and grime.

If you can't be bothered washing your duvet, at least hang it on the clothes line in the sun to allow the UV rays to kill bacteria.

HINT

Mosquitoes in the middle of the night
You're lying in bed, half asleep, when a high-pitched buzzing begins somewhere near your ear. The dreaded mozzie! You start whacking your face in the vain hope of killing it. But if the noise stops, it generally means one thing: you're being bitten. The best solution is lavender oil. Keep a bottle beside your bed. When you hear buzzing, put a drop on your pillowcase and another drop on your hands, then rub it all over your body and face. A couple of drops is enough for one person. You could even put a couple of drops in a spray bottle of water and spray it over you and the bed before going to sleep. Lavender oil has the triple purpose of keeping mosquitoes away, soothing the bite and assisting with sleep. I've even used a novelty spray fan to help deal with the problem.

Blankets

Blankets should be aired regularly, preferably once a week, and outside if possible. Woollen blankets should be washed once every 4–6 months in shampoo and conditioner – the cheaper, the better, because they contain less perfume. For single-sized blankets, use 3 dessertspoons of shampoo with water warmed to blood temperature, rinse, then use 3 dessertspoons of conditioner with water warmed to blood temperature. Use double the amount for double-sized blankets. After rinsing, dry them in the morning sun or dappled shade, not the afternoon sun, or the blankets will stiffen.

Machine wash only if the manufacturer's instructions indicate that you can. If you use the washing machine, add 1–1½ caps of woolwash for a double blanket. If you wash the blanket in the bath, use 2 caps of woolwash or shampoo. Don't leave blankets to soak. Just wash them in blood-heat water, rinse in blood-heat water and hang to dry. If you agitate woollen blankets too much, the blanket will shrink, leaving you with a felt wad instead of a soft blanket.

Cotton blankets can be machine washed the same way as sheets. Faux mink blankets can be hand washed with woolwash or shampoo in blood-heat water. Make sure you brush with a hairbrush as it dries. Polar fleece blankets are made from recycled plastic bags and are best cleaned with washing powder or liquid.

Never put sheepskin in the washing machine or agitate it. Instead, wash sheepskin underblankets with woolwash or shampoo in a bath, sink or bucket. Dry them lying flat. Just before the sheepskin is completely dry, brush it with a hairbrush in all directions.

Read the washing instructions before cleaning an electric blanket. If it doesn't have any instructions, take it to a reputable dry cleaner.

If you have space, store blankets in a blanket box or, better still, a camphor wood box because this will keep insects away. Otherwise, keep blankets in the cupboard but protect them with some camphor inside a handkerchief and plastic bag. Prick little holes in the plastic and put it inside your blankets. This will keep insects and other nasties away but won't mark your blankets. Store duvets the same way.

HINT

This may seem excessive but it's a good habit to get into. Strip your bed every day, let it air for at least 2 minutes, then remake the bed with the same sheets. Air pillows once a week either outside in the sun or over a chair near the window. UV is great at killing bacteria. Fluff the pillows up before returning them to the bed. Your bed will feel drier and fresher everyday, not just when you change the sheets. If you can easily fold a pillow in half, it's time for a new one!

DRAWERS AND WARDROBES

Drawers and wardrobes take many forms. They can be built-in or stand alone, old or new. Those with a shellac, French polish or varnish finish should be cleaned once a month with a good quality, silicone-free furniture polish. Just put a small amount of polish on a cloth, wipe it over the piece, then wipe it off with the other side of the cloth. A good furniture polish should remove most small scratches.

Those with a laminate or polyurethane finish can be cleaned with a damp cloth. If they're very dirty, use bicarb and white vinegar. Keep polyurethane pieces away from windows because the sun's UV rays will yellow them.

To clean the inside of drawers, take your clothes out and vacuum. If the area is very dirty, use white vinegar and water on a sponge. To deter nasties, put some lavender oil or tea tree oil on a cloth and wipe over the drawer or cupboard interior. A cake of soap left in the drawer will also deter insects and scent your clothes. You can also buy scented and anti-insect drawer liners to fit into your drawers. These will also protect your clothes from the tannins in the wood.

If you apply make-up at a dressing table with a wooden surface, protect it with a glass tile or mirror tile. A mirror tile is preferable

because it gives backlighting and your make-up
perfectly. I also like to put foam in my bedside table
if I drop make-up bottles or jewellery, they won't break

Stand wardrobes at least 10 cm from the wall so that a.
circulate. If you have more than one wardrobe, stand them a.
apart as possible to maximise air circulation. If this isn't possible,
stand them right next to each other so you don't create difficult-to-
access dust corridors. Make sure wardrobe doors can be opened
completely so you can easily reach inside. Don't forget to wipe a
damp cloth over the tops of wardrobes. The dust that gathers here
eventually makes its way around the room so it's important to clean
here too.

Clothes last longer if they're hung rather than folded, so hang as
much as you can. The exception is woollens and knits, which should
be stored flat. Use good coathangers. Wooden hangers are the best,
plastic are OK and wire coathangers need to be wrapped with foam
strips or have old shoulder pads pinned on the shoulders of the hanger.

DID YOU KNOW? To deter moths, silverfish, dust mites and
other insects, place 1 camphor ball, 4 cloves, a head of
lavender, a couple of drops of eucalyptus oil and 2 bay
leaves in a small muslin bag, tie it, then hang it on the
rod in your wardrobe. It will also make your clothes smell
fresh and lovely!

Drawer liners

There is a perception that drawer liners are very last century, but I
think they're a great protection for clothes. Not only do they deter
silverfish and mould, they also keep your clothes smelling fresh.
Modern drawers generally aren't finished well and clothes can catch
on splinters or rough plastic lugs. Use liners and you'll cut back on

...ne spent mending! All you have to do is place them on the bottom of each drawer in your chest of drawers. You can either buy them or make your own.

To make your own drawer liners, buy some acid-free paper from an art supplies shop. Acid-free paper will prevent yellowing in clothes. Fill a spray bottle with warm water, add 1 tea bag and leave for 3 minutes. Remove the tea bag and add a couple of drops of oil of cloves and some of your favourite perfume, then spray over the paper. This mixture is particularly good for winter woollens and the tannins from the tea help prevent dust mites. Allow the paper to dry, then cut it to size and place it in your drawers. Replace them once a year. You could even match your draw liners to your bedroom's decoration scheme, as my mother does!

Problem:	**Sticking drawers in furniture.**
What to use:	**Soap or candle wax/Gumption, sponge.**
How to apply:	Take the drawer out. If it has wooden runners, rub them with soap. You can also rub candle wax along the runners. For plastic runners, polish with Gumption on a sponge. If this doesn't work, your chest of drawers may be uneven. You can check this with a spirit level horizontally and vertically. If it is not level, put some cardboard or a small block of wood under one of the legs to steady it. You could also have a problem with the backing sheet of the drawer, which may need to be refastened or replaced if it's buckled. A lot of modern furniture is built with cheap backing sheets and if they buckle it takes the drawers out of alignment. It's easy to check this by looking at the back of the drawer and making sure the sheets are flush to the edge. You can replace them yourself or get professional help. Also check

that the joints of the drawer are secure. If you're
re-painting your drawers, don't paint the sides of
each drawer or they will stick!

Problem:	**Moths in the wardrobe.**
What to use:	**Camphor ball, cloves, lavender, eucalyptus oil, small muslin bag.**
How to apply:	Place 1 camphor ball, 4 cloves, a sprig of lavender and a couple of drops of eucalyptus oil into a small muslin bag. Tie it, then hang it on the rod in your wardrobe. Replace eucalyptus and lavender every two months. Replace the others yearly.

Q: 'When you've had your clothes sitting on a coathanger for a while, the hanger can leave a mark,' reports Terzine. 'If you don't have time to iron it out, is there anything you can do?'

Problem:	**Hanger marks on clothes.**
What to use:	**Spray bottle, body heat.**
How to apply:	Before you put the garment on, damp spray the spot with water where the hanger has left its indentation. When you put the garment on, your body heat will interact with the water and smooth the marks out. To prevent the problem, wrap the shoulder line of your coathanger with foam strips or old shoulder pads.

CLOTHING

My mother has a horror of anything that itches – and she passed
this on to me in spades. Clothes have to be soft on your skin and

finished properly. Of course you're going to get spills and stains on your clothes; they're a barrier between you and the world. Start by working out what's in the stain. If it has several components, remove proteins first, then fats, then chemicals.

To help, as soon as you remove your dirty clothes, put them straight into a laundry basket. For clothes you'll wear again, get into the habit of putting them away in the wardrobe, not leaving them on the floor or letting them pile up on a chair. In fact, if you hang clothes while they're still warm, they won't need ironing because the heat will iron out the creases. If there are any stains, deal with them as soon as you can. They're harder to clean once they've set.

If there's mending to do, such as sewing a hem or replacing a button, do this before you wash. If you don't, the job will become larger. I have a dedicated sewing basket and mend during the evening while watching TV. If you don't mend garments yourself, create a pile to take to a professional. Mending services are often available at laundrettes and dry cleaners and can sometimes be found right next door to shops that sell suits.

Q: 'My cotton business shirts have sweat stains that just won't wash out,' says Steve. 'Do you have a suggestion on what to do because the shirts aren't cheap!'

Problem:	**Sweat marks on fabric.**
What to use:	**Vanish Oxi Action.**
How to apply:	Make a paste with Vanish Oxi Action and water to the consistency of peanut butter and apply this to the stain. Leave for 15 minutes before washing. You must use Vanish Oxi Action rather than just Vanish.

Q: 'My deodorant has left white stains on my shirts,' says Susie. 'It's like it's permanently caked on now. Can I remove this?'

Problem:	Deodorant stains on fabric.
What to use:	Vanish Oxi Action.
How to apply:	Make a paste with Vanish Oxi Action and water to the consistency of peanut butter. Apply it to the deodorant stains and leave for 15 minutes, then wash the shirts as usual in the washing machine.

Q: 'My husband was wearing suntan cream and it's marked the neckline of his shirt,' says Sandra. 'Can I get it off?'

Problem:	Suntan cream on fabric.
What to use:	Washing up liquid/Vanish Oxi Action, water.
How to apply:	Place a couple of drops of washing up liquid on your fingers and rub into the stain until it changes texture and feels like jelly. Leave for 15 minutes and wash and dry normally. Alternatively, soak in Vanish Oxi Action and water for 15 minutes, then wash and dry normally. The latter works better with self-tanning creams.

Q: 'I'm a bachelor,' says Geoffrey. 'And I accidentally put my jumper into the washing machine and it's shrunk. Can it be fixed?'

Problem:	Shrunken jumper.
What to use:	Bucket, Fuller's Earth, towel, two wide-toothed combs/Epsom salts.

How to apply: For dark-coloured jumpers, fill a nappy-sized bucket
with blood-heat water and add 2 tablespoons of
Fuller's Earth. For light-coloured jumpers, add 4
tablespoons. Put the jumper in and gently agitate it
with your hands until it's thoroughly wetted. Let it sit
for 10–15 minutes and then rinse thoroughly in
blood-heat water. Don't leave it for longer than this
or it will bleach. Lie the jumper flat on a towel in a
shady spot and leave it to dry. Gently stretch it back
into shape as it's drying. To make it stretch more
evenly, use two wide-toothed combs on either side
of the jumper and stretch the jumper with the combs
as it's drying. It's not as effective, but you could also
use 2 tablespoons of Epsom salts, instead of Fuller's
Earth, in a bucket of blood-heat water.

Q: 'I hate the dressing on new shirts,' says Stephen. 'Is
there a way you can soften them so they're like
your old favourite shirts?'

Problem: How to soften stiff or brand new shirts.
What to use: Bicarb, washing powder, white vinegar.
How to apply: Put the shirts through the washing machine, adding
60 g of bicarb to your washing powder and 120 ml of
white vinegar to the rinse water.

Q: 'I pulled out an old cream satin evening gown
which was covered in mildew,' says Barbara. 'Is it
fixable?'

Problem: Mildew on satin.
What to use: Hairdryer, clothes brush, salt.

How to apply: Blow a hairdryer over the satin until it is warm. This causes the mildew to blow up and fluff up. Then rub a clothes brush in the direction of the watery-looking part of the satin. If any black marks remain, cover them with dry salt and brush backwards and forwards with a clothes brush. Then brush off.

Problem: Stretched cotton-knit jumper.
What to use: Wide-toothed comb, Fuller's Earth.
How to apply: Use a wide-toothed comb to evenly stretch the jumper. Then put it in the washing machine on the hot water setting. Before it reaches the spin cycle, remove the jumper and put it in the dryer. The water superheats and shrinks the fibres. You can also add 1 tablespoon of Fuller's Earth to the wash cycle to help shrink it.

How to stop angora jumpers shedding

To stop angora jumpers from shedding, put them in the freezer for 20 minutes before wearing them. Or add a little hair conditioner the size of a 10-pence piece to the rinse water when you're washing them.

Q: 'How do you remove chocolate ice cream from a T-shirt?' asks Maureen.

Problem: Chocolate ice-cream on T-shirt.
What to use: Bar of soap.
How to apply: As the chocolate contains protein, you must use cold water. Vigorously rub the stain with the soap and cold water. Then wash normally.

Problem: Shine on a suit.

What to use: Cloth, white vinegar, unprocessed wheat bran, brown paper, iron.

How to apply: For a dark-coloured suit, dampen a cloth in white vinegar and wipe it over the suit. Then place brown paper over the suit and iron. For light-coloured suits, dampen a cloth in 1 part white vinegar to 4 parts water, wring it out and lay it over the shiny section of the suit. Steam-iron the suit.

Q: 'My daughter works as a beauty therapist,' says Sandra, 'and she waxes a lot of legs. As a consequence, her black synthetic slacks have wax on them. How should I get it off?'

Problem: Wax on synthetic fabric.

What to use: Paper towel, hairdryer.

How to apply: Put a paper towel on either side of the wax and blow a hairdryer over the area. The paper towel will absorb the wax. Keep on replacing the paper towel until the wax is removed.

Q: 'My six-year-old daughter wore her brand new white ladybird T-shirt under a walnut tree,' says Megan, 'and bird dropping landed on her. What can I do?'

Problem: Bird dropping on fabric.

What to use: White vinegar, glycerine, salt, Vanish.

How to apply: Walnuts contain a dye that has to be treated with white vinegar first, then glycerine. Soak the fabric until the stain begins to move. Rub with glycerine, then salt. Rinse, then wash in Vanish.

Q: 'I work in the transport industry,' says Tom, 'and I'm always getting grease on my clothes. What should I do?'

Problem:	**Old car grease/engine oil on fabric.**
What to use:	**Baby oil, washing up liquid, water.**
How to apply:	Car grease has a high carbon content, so rub the stain with a dab of baby oil. As soon as the stain starts to loosen and spread, massage in washing up liquid with your fingers. When it feels like jelly, rinse in water.

Q: 'I used to get rust off my sailing clothes with a product called Rustyban,' reports David. 'It was taken off the market and I'm wondering what I can use now.'

Problem:	**Rust on fabric.**
What to use:	**Cotton wool ball, cotton bud, descaler/lemon juice and salt.**
How to apply:	Try descaler instead. Put a cotton wool ball behind the stain and dip a cotton bud in descaler. Rub it over the rust until it starts to lift. Then hand wash the garment straight away – the rust should come off. Descaler is a very strong product so be careful. If you'd rather use something natural, try lemon juice and salt. Dampen the rust spot with lemon juice and then rub salt over it until the rust starts to move from the fibres. Hand wash and begin the process again until all the rust comes out. This could take some time.

: 'When I was travelling, the blue from my asthma pack rubbed onto my yellow polyester viscose trousers,' says Jocelynne. 'Can I get it off?'

Problem: **Ink stain on fabric.**
What to use: **Milk.**
How to apply: Rot a carton of milk in the sun and spread the solids over the stain. Leave until the ink begins to rise into the milk solids. Then wash the rotten milk out in the washing machine.

Q: 'I buy a lot of second-hand clothes,' says Joyce. 'But they often have a musty smell about them. What do you suggest?'

Problem: **Musty smell on clothes.**
What to use: **Tea bag.**
How to apply: The musty smell is caused by dust mites and mildew. To get rid of it, put a tea bag into the washing machine after the water has filled, but before it starts agitating. Hold the bag in the water for 2 minutes then remove. The tannins in the tea kill dust mites. If you suffer dust mite allergy, keep a damp tea bag in a plastic bag in your handbag to sniff when you're in second-hand stores. It'll stop you from sneezing.

Problem: **Dirty woollen coats, dresses or skirts.**
What to use: **Salt, clean handkerchief or piece of linen, bristle brush.**
How to apply: This is an alternative to dry cleaning and much cheaper. Sprinkle the item with salt about as thickly

as poppy seeds on bread. Then rub with a clean
handkerchief or piece of linen. Don't go in circles but
up and down with the grain of the fabric. Once the
item is clean, give it a really good shake and brush
with a bristle brush.

Q: 'My mum gave me her old mink jacket,' says Jo.
'I have no idea how to clean it.'

Problem:	**Cleaning fur or faux fur coats.**
What to use:	**Pillowcase, wheat bran.**
How to apply:	Place the coat in a large pillowcase and add 1 kg of bran. Secure the top of the pillowcase and shake vigorously for about 3 minutes. Open the pillowcase and lightly shake the item as you remove it, so the bran stays in the pillowcase. This technique is also good for wool, mohair or camel coats and is a quick way to clean suits.

Silk

The best way to wash silk is with shampoo and with conditioner in
the rinse water. Use the same amount as you would with your hair.
Never dry silk on a windy day because all the fibres go stiff and
cause white dusty marks, white lines and water marks.

Problem:	**Water marks on silk.**
What to use:	**Clean white silk square.**
How to apply:	As taught to me by my grandmother, rub the clean white silk square gently across and down the grain of the silk. Don't rub diagonally.

Problem: White lines on silk.
What to use: White vinegar, salt.
How to apply: When hand washing silk, put white vinegar into the rinse water and the white lines won't appear. To keep silk soft, put a teaspoon of salt in the washing water.

Q: 'I splashed black coffee over my favourite silk tie,' says Geoff. 'It just won't shift!'

Problem: Coffee stain on silk.
What to use: Glycerine, cotton wool ball, washing power, white vinegar, towel.
How to apply: Apply glycerine to the stain with a cotton wool ball. Then wash the tie with washing powder in blood-heat water. Rinse in blood-heat water and, to prevent the tie stiffening, add a little white vinegar. Then dry it flat on a towel in the shade.

Leather

Problem: Oily stains on suede.
What to use: Wheat bran, white vinegar.
How to apply: You can clean suede by rubbing bran over it. Remove sweat marks by dampening some white vinegar on the marks, then rub with bran.

How to repair a small hole in a leather jacket

Most people have a leather jacket for life unless it was one of those bat-wing 1980s numbers. Getting a hole is usually devastating, but here's how you can keep the jacket alive.

Find a matching piece of leather. This could be taken from the inside of the hemline or seam or under an armpit seam. Cut a paper template 1 millimetre larger than the shape of the hole, place it on top of the leather piece and cut around it to make the patch. Sand the back of the leather patch with sandpaper so that you thin the edges. On a piece of linen or cotton that is 1 cm larger all round than the leather patch apply malleable contact adhesive or specialist leather adhesive and glue on the patch.

The patch will now be sitting in the middle of the sticky, adhesive-covered piece of linen or cotton. Line the patch up with the back of the hole and attach. You'll find it's a little thick where the two layers overlap. Lay the face of the leather on a smooth surface such as a breadboard and tap the back of it with a flat-headed hammer. The leather will smooth out and appear to be one piece of leather again.

Turn it over again so you're looking at the front. Warm a spoon, dip the back of it in a little Vaseline and lightly rub the patched area. For hard leather surfaces, use paraffin wax.

Zips

Problem:	**Sticky zips.**
What to use:	**White vinegar, lead pencil, graphite powder/glycerine, talcum powder.**
How to apply:	For metal zips, apply some white vinegar to the zip then rub the metal with a lead pencil or apply graphite powder. Work it up and down. Graphite isn't as effective as a lead pencil, because it doesn't contain clay, but it will work with a little persistence. For nylon zips, apply some glycerine, working it up and down. Then sprinkle with talcum powder.

Problem: Loose zips.
What to use: Salt.
How to apply: To make zips stick, add a little salt to them. This works with both metal or nylon zips.

Q: 'The zip on my sailing jacket has salt build-up on it,' says William. 'Can it be fixed?'

Problem: Salt on metal zip.
What to use: Cloth, white vinegar, lead pencil.
How to apply: Wipe the zip with a cloth dipped in white vinegar first, then rub it with a lead pencil.

BAGS

The great thing about a bag is you don't have go on a diet to wear one. They really are 'one size fits all'! I love handbags that can store as much as possibl: the bigger the better and the more the merrier. Store bags in a cool dry place covered in a calico bag or old pillowcase.

Problem: Smelly leather handbag/suitcase.
What to use: Tea leaves, leather conditioner.
How to apply: The bag may smell because it wasn't tanned properly or is made of goat or kangaroo hide. To get rid of the smell, wipe the leather with damp tea leaves. This will cure the leather. Then treat it with leather conditioner. If the interior of the bag is made of leather and also smells, empty a packet of dry tea leaves into it and leave for a couple of weeks.

Problem:	**Mouldy handbag.**
What to use:	**White vinegar, cloths, oil of cloves, leather conditioner.**
How to apply:	Mix a small quantity of white vinegar and water and wipe it over the mould with a cloth. Then wipe with a clean cloth. Add 1 drop of oil of cloves to leather conditioner on a cloth and wipe over the bag. The oil of cloves will inhibit further mould growth.

Problem:	**Dirty handbag lining.**
What to use:	**Washing powder.**
How to apply:	Some bag linings can be removed. Others are attached but can still be pulled outside the bag. If the lining is cotton, clean it with washing powder and water. To dry, put the leather part of the bag in the shade and the lining in the sun. If you can't do this, dry the whole bag in the shade. The lining must be completely dry before you put it back inside the bag.

SHOES

If you're feeling lazy about looking after your shoes, just think about how much it will cost to replace them. Store very good shoes in a shoe bag or calico bag to stop them from going mouldy. After wearing leather and vinyl shoes, dust the insides of them with a little bicarb. Wipe the outside with a cloth that's been smeared with Vaseline. Bicarb reduces the amount of sweat your feet produces and the Vaseline makes shoes waterproof. Just don't forget to dust out the bicarb before you wear the shoes again.

Dust bicarb into cloth and running shoes and vacuum it out before wearing them. Most cloth shoes can be hand or machine washed. Sprinkle talcum powder on rubber soles and the outside of rubber boots to stop them perishing.

Spray suede and cloth shoes with Scotchgard to keep them clean for longer, and waterproof. For nubuck or super suede shoes, purchase a small proprietary brand sandblock for cleaning.

Keep the ankles of boots unwrinkled and firm by putting an old paper towel roll inside them so they don't flop over.

Make sure you use the correct shoelaces on shoes. If they're too thin, you place strain on the holes. If they're too thick, you place strain on the front of the shoe. The lace should move through the hole with a light resistance, not a drag nor a run.

If you get a hole in the sole of your shoe, put newspaper on the inside of the sole and use a product called Spread-a-sole. Apply it in several thin coats and it will form a new sole.

If nail heads are coming through your shoes it means your heels may need to be replaced or boosted. Hammer the nails back in, making sure you cover the head of the nail with a small piece of wood.

Problem:	**Rubber soles are perishing.**
What to use:	**Salt, stiff brush.**
How to apply:	Scour the rubber with salt and a stiff brush. This will rejuvenate them.

Problem:	**Velcro not working.**
What to use:	**Fine-toothed comb.**
How to apply:	Dampen the Velcro with water and comb it on both sides with a fine-toothed comb. This gets the fluff and dust out.

How to care for stockings
You wouldn't bother doing this with cheap stockings, but it's worth it with expensive ones. Put soap in one toe and your hand in the other toe and then rub them together as though you're washing your hands. This stretches the fibres and removes more dirt.

HATS

I collect hats in many different styles, from Georgian to contemporary. I even have a pop-up silk top hat! Special hats should be stored in a hatbox or on a hat block and kept on a flat surface. If the hat has a high crown and you don't have a hat block, pack it with acid-free tissue paper. Hand wash woollen berets in woolwash and dry them over a dinner plate so they retain their shape.

Problem: Sweat marks on felt hats.
What to use: Fuller's Earth or plaster of Paris, paintbrush, brush.
How to apply: Sweat on light-coloured hats can be removed with Fuller's Earth. Mix Fuller's Earth and water to the consistency of soft butter. Then paint it over the sweat marks with a paintbrush, leave to dry and then brush out. For dark-coloured felt hats use plaster of Paris made to the consistency of soft butter. Put the mixture over the sweat stain with a paintbrush and allow it to dry completely before brushing it off.

Problem: Straw hat has gone floppy.
What to use: Pastry brush, egg white, towels, cling film.
How to apply: Dip a pastry brush in egg white and wipe both sides of the hat with it. Put towels in the crown of the hat, cover a flat surface with cling film, sit the hat on top and allow it to dry hard.

Q: 'I'm a fan of felt hats,' says Simon, 'but mine seems to have shrunk. Can it be stretched?'

Problem:	**Felt hat has shrunk.**
What to use:	**Fuller's Earth, hat block or damp newspaper.**
How to apply:	Mix Fuller's Earth and water to the consistency of peanut butter. Spread it over the areas that need to be stretched and leave for about 5 minutes. Then force the hat over a suitably sized hat block or pack the inside of the crown with damp newspaper until it's the right size. Leave to dry in the shade, not the sun. The drying time will depend on the thickness of the hat.

JEWELLERY

Use nothing more than a little water to clean absorbent precious stones such as jade, opal, some agates, cloudy quartz and emerald.

Pearls should only be cleaned in a mild salt solution – 1 teaspoon of salt for 600 millilitres of water.

Ivory can be cleaned with sweet almond oil on a cotton bud. Other jewellery should be cleaned with a proprietary product.

Never use heat or chemicals on jewellery. If in doubt, take it to a jeweller.

Jewellery boxes

Clean jewellery boxes as you would other furniture. The easiest way to clean the inside is to vacuum it. Just make sure you cover the vacuum cleaner tube with an old T-shirt just in case you suck up a stone! I came up with this solution after dropping about 30 small gemstones that had all been collected from old pieces of jewellery on a multicoloured, long-pile carpet. The stones are now a gorgeous necklace!

CHILDREN'S BEDROOMS

Help your children get into good cleaning habits. Keep a dirty clothes' basket in their room and show them how to use it. Place beds away from the wall so they can tuck the sheets in. Attach labels to drawers with pictures of what's inside to help them sort their clothes. Use plastic tubs to store toys. Create a specific area to do homework and creative pursuits. Have simple shelving units and lots of them. Keep a big wastepaper bin in the room.

If your child is a constant vomiter, keep a bucket or bowl in their bedroom with fresh towels for instant mop ups. If you catch vomit in a bucket and with a towel, it makes cleaning much easier. You could also use a wastepaper bin with a solid bottom. Do whatever you can to stop vomit getting into the mattress. Rinse the soiled towel first then put it through the washing machine.

CHAPTER 8:
Outside

The garden used to be just a patch of lawn, a shed and a clothes line. These days you've got tiles, paving stones, decks, barbecues, fences, feature walls, pool surrounds and the rest of the landscaping to look after. Fortunately, much of it can be weather-proofed and spill-proofed so you can play, entertain and tinker with ease.

ASSEMBLE THE CLEAN KIT

bicarb – cleaning agent
black tea bags – to protect outdoor furniture and freshen air
cider white vinegar – cleaning agent
clutter bucket – to transport displaced items
detergent (washing up liquid) – cleaning agent
disposable rubber gloves – to protect hands
dustpan and brush – to clean up accumulated dirt
lemon oil and peel – to deter spiders
long-handled soft nylon broom – to remove spider webs
nylon broom – to sweep
oil of cloves – to deter mould
straw broom – to sweep
sweet almond oil – to lubricate
table salt – cleaning agent
talcum powder – to protect rubber

CLEANING SPECIFIC TO OUTSIDE

Clear everything that doesn't belong with a clutter bucket. Remove spider webs by running a long-handled broom over them. Collect as much web as you can over the broom. Then put on disposable rubber gloves and use the rubber to grip the webs free from the broom. Throw the web-coated gloves in the bin. Rinse the broom in water and set in the sun to dry.

HINT **DID YOU KNOW?** If you leave spider webs for too long, moisture in the webs can affect paintwork and make it flake. Deter spiders by rubbing lemon peel over the area. It will help if you put a little lemon oil on the broom bristles before you wipe the spider webs away – you'll do both jobs in one clean sweep!

Sweep pathways with a good straw or garden broom. I use straw brooms because they're stiffer and more abrasive. Place old leaves and dirt in a dustpan and put straight into your garden waste recycling bin. I have a dustpan with a long handle and an attached broom to save on bending. If you have wooden decking, sweep with the broom. Never use detergent on unsealed wood because it will dry it out and splinter. Instead, use water and 120 ml of cider white vinegar. If the area is very dirty, sprinkle a little bicarb on first, splash cider white vinegar over the top, then scrub with a nylon broom while it's fizzing.

Keep an eye on your exterior paintwork. If there's any peeling paint, sweep over it regularly because moisture can get in and make the peeling spot even bigger. It's much better to have a chip than a peeling edge.

Clean under eaves and awnings and around light fittings with a nylon broom. Spiders love light fittings, but their webs are conductive and can short your lights! Add a little lemon oil to the brush of your broom and wipe over the lights to deter spiders.

WOODEN DECKING

Whether you should seal wood depends on the wood. Some woods such as teak, oak and treated cedar can handle exposure to the elements. But, if you don't want it to wear or change colour, treat it with tung oil or a good outdoor sealant. If you have timber from the 1970s get rid of it because most were treated with copper and arsenic and are toxic. Remove them with great care.

There are some significant differences between cleaning sealed and unsealed wood and, if you mix them up, you'll be in trouble. Clean sealed wood with 3 teaspoons of washing-up liquid in a bucket of warm water. Use a broom rather than a mop because it can reach into all the crevices.

Again, don't use detergent on unsealed wood because it dries it out and causes splinters. Unsealed wood should be cleaned with 1 bucket of warm water and 240 ml of white vinegar and a couple of drops of eucalyptus oil. The eucalyptus oil both cleans and feeds the wood. But don't use eucalyptus oil on painted surfaces because it's a paint stripper. Dilute a pot of strong tea (use 4–5 tea bags) in a bucket of hot water and mop the wood. This will help prevent it going that silvery colour.

 'We love spending time on the outside deck,' reports Paul. 'But so do some foxes. What's the best way to deal with fox poo?'

Problem:	**Fox poo on decking.**
What to use:	**Soap froth, cold water, stiff broom.**
How to apply:	Fox poo is high in protein because foxes are carnivorous and eat plenty of meat. Remove the protein part of the stain first with soap froth and cold water. You must use cold water or you'll set the protein. Apply the soap froth with a stiff broom then rinse with water. If the area is exposed to sunlight, shade it with an umbrella while you're cleaning because heat will set fox poo.

BRICKS AND TERRACOTTA PAVING STONES

Bricks and pavers can be cleaned with bicarb and white vinegar.
Sprinkle the bicarb then splash white vinegar over the top. Wipe it
down with a stiff broom then rinse with water. To deter mould and
algae, add a couple of drops of oil of cloves to the rinse water. If you
want to encourage mould and mosses, add yoghurt to the rinse water.

Problem:	**Masonry beetle in the mortar.**
What to use:	**WD-40.**
How to apply:	Use the extension nozzle on the WD-40 and spray into the holes dug by the masonry beetle. This kills them.

GLAZED TILES

Clean tiles with a mild solution of washing up liquid. If your tiles
have a tendency to become slippery, create a non-skid surface by
adding white vinegar to the rinse water. Seal terracotta or Spanish
quarry tiles with a proprietary product or make your own temporary
sealant with 1 part Unibond PVA to 20 parts water. Apply with a
mop. (Make sure you wash the mop with soap and water
afterwards or it will stiffen.) If the tiles are particularly slippery, mop
the floor then scatter a small amount of sand over the surface, then
mop again. I did exactly this at my doctor's surgery because I was
worried someone would slip on the sloping tiled path. It lasts for
about three months.

 Q: 'I've got some lovely camellia plants and palms in
my courtyard,' reports Shirley. 'But the petals and
leaves are leaving dark stains on the ceramic tiles.
Is there a solution?'

Problem: Plant stains on tiles.

What to use: Effervescent denture tablet, wet cloth/bicarb, white vinegar, brush, mop.

How to apply: Place 1 effervescent denture tablet on the stain and then place a wet cloth over the top and leave overnight. Alternatively, sprinkle bicarb and splash white vinegar over the area with a brush, scrub and leave for two hours. Then rinse with a mop and water.

STONE AND SANDSTONE

The best way to clean stone and sandstone is with the pool-cleaning product Surex 002 Oxysure. Surex is an alternative to chlorine and doesn't kill plants like chlorine does. Use 1 cap of Surex per bucket of water and apply with a broom. Leave it for a couple of hours then rinse with water. Add a couple of drops of oil of cloves to the rinse water to inhibit mould, or add yoghurt to encourage mould and mosses.

 'I've got some purple droppings on my sandstone patio,' reports Shelly. 'I think it's from a bird. Can I get rid of them?'

Problem: Bird droppings on sandstone.

What to use: Nothing.

How to apply: In most cases, bird droppings will fade in sunlight over time.

CONCRETE

Concrete is best cleaned with bicarb and white vinegar. Sprinkle the bicarb over the surface, splash the white vinegar on top and scrub with a broom. Then rinse with water. To stop leaves staining the concrete and to make grease removal easier, seal concrete with a proprietary product or with a temporary sealant of 1 part Unibond PVA to 20 parts water. Apply with a mop. Make sure you rinse your mop afterwards or it will stiffen.

Problem:	**Ivy suckers stuck on concrete/brick.**
What to use:	**Heat gun, stiff brush.**
How to apply:	Apply a heat gun to the suckers until they go hard. Allow them to cool and dry, then scrub them off with a stiff brush.

HINT

Doormats
I always have a mat at the front and back doors of the house. It's also a good idea to have mats on the inside to prevent dirt tracking into the house. If you don't want to use a mat inside, spray the carpet regularly with Scotchgard. It's also handy to have a shoe cupboard near the back door for dirty wellies. Alternatively, go old-fashioned and use a boot scraper.

WINDOWS

Cleaning the outsides of windows is a spring/autumn-cleaning job and I think it's best left to a professional.

OUTDOOR FURNITURE

Outdoor furniture can be made of sealed or unsealed wood, aluminium, glass, plastic, cane or polycarbonate.

To clean sealed wood, use a mild detergent solution. Many outdoor settings are made of red cedar, which can be cleaned with water. Re-stain it every three years. Painted surfaces should be cleaned in a mild washing up liquid solution.

To clean unsealed wood, add 240 ml of white vinegar and a couple of drops of eucalyptus oil to a bucket of water and wipe with a cloth.

To clean aluminium settings, use bicarb and white vinegar. You could also try cold black tea! I discovered this recently when I accidentally spilled some tea over aluminium meshing and it came up like glass! Have one sponge with bicarb on it and another soaked in white vinegar. Press the white vinegar sponge through the bicarb sponge and wipe. You can remove water marks the same way.

To clean polycarbonate or plastic, use a mild solution of washing up liquid. Don't confuse polycarbonate with polyacetate or polyurethane. It's best not to leave opaque polycarbonate in the sun because it becomes weak and a chair may collapse while you're sitting in it – as happened to me at a party one time.

To clean cane and wicker, scrub with soap and water, leave in the sun to dry and seal with shellac or a good outdoor sealant. Spray the sealant on if possible with a plastic spray bottle.

Some outdoor chairs are made of shade cloth and should be washed regularly with mild soapy water. Wash them after it rains because they collect mildew. Where possible, keep outdoor cushions under cover when you're not using them. If cushions do get wet in the rain, wash them because they'll collect mildew. Add a couple of drops of oil of cloves to the rinse water to inhibit mould. Chairs not in use should be stored under cover on an angle. A potential hazard with outdoor furniture is the nasty surprises that take up residence under the table. Keep spiders away by regularly wiping some lemon oil on the underside of it.

You need to clean outdoor furniture only when it's dirty or to tidy up before friends visit. There's nothing worse than a guest standing up to find dirt all over their new white linen trousers!

Problem:	**Outdoor furniture has gone grey in the sun.**
What to use:	**Strong solution of tea, varnish.**
How to apply:	Wash it with a strong solution of tea before re-varnishing it.

Problem:	**Rust on cast iron.**
What to use:	**White vinegar, wire brush, rust converter.**
How to apply:	Loosen the rust with white vinegar then scrub with a wire brush. Then apply rust converter. This produces a hard surface that you can then repaint.

UMBRELLAS, AWNINGS AND SHADE CLOTH

These are essential in a hot summer. Clean canvas with 450 g of salt added to a small bucket of water and apply with a brush or broom. Leave to dry then rinse the salt away. Umbrellas are best left up so they don't hoard insects. If they are down, keep them wrapped in a cover. To clean canvas umbrellas, put 450 g of table salt or swimming pool salt in a small bucket of water and apply to the canvas with a brush or stiff broom. Allow it to dry then brush the salt crust off with a dry broom.

Clean plastic with water. If it's very dirty, add some washing up liquid to the water.

Raffia umbrellas attract insects so hose or wash them regularly and spray with surface insecticide.

Metal poles can be cleaned with graphite. Rust and plastic attachments can be cleaned with glycerine.

Problem:	**Mildew on canvas.**
What to use:	**Strong salt solution, bucket, brush or broom, oil of cloves, spray bottle.**
How to apply:	Scrub the canvas with 450 g of salt added to a small bucket of water and apply with a brush or broom. Leave it to dry. There should be a lot of salt on the surface. Scrub it again to help loosen any remaining mildew. Hose or wash it clean in a sunny spot. Then spray the canvas with a few drops of oil of cloves and water in a spray pack. This will prevent the mildew returning.
	To clean mildew on canvas add 1 kg of table salt per bucket of water. Sweep it on with a broom, leave it to dry and then sweep it off with a stiff broom. Rinse with water if necessary, adding a couple of drops of oil of cloves to inhibit mould growth.

GUTTERS, DRAINS, EAVES AND AWNINGS

Get into the habit of checking your gutters three times a year. When leaves collect in gutters, they hold moisture in one spot causing corrosion and rust. And anyone who's had to replace gutters knows it's not a cheap exercise! With gloves and a bucket, climb a ladder and scoop the leaves out handful by handful into the bucket until all the leaves are cleared. You can avoid this tedious job by fitting a dome mesh guard in your gutters, which are easy to install. The guard causes most leaves to fall over and onto the ground – those leaves that do become lodged can be cleared easily by running a

broom along the gutter. Once on the ground, simply sweep the
leaves up and put them in the garden waste recycling bin.

HINT

Always have mesh over drains and check they're in
working order – and be careful what you put down them.
If you have a grease trap, make sure it is cleaned by
professionals.

DID YOU KNOW? Clear a blocked drain by putting 50 g of
bicarb down the pipe, then pour in 240 ml white vinegar and
leave for a few minutes. Flush with hot water: just boil the kettle
and pour it down.

HINT

Caring for rubber
Never leave anything made of rubber sitting in the
sunshine. This includes flippers, masks, trays or seats. To
prevent rubber perishing, rub it with talcum powder after
cleaning. If it has perished, rub some salt on the perished
area then dust with talcum powder. The salt acts as a
sander.

BARBECUES

Barbecue hotplates are made of cast iron and should be cleaned
after each use. It's preferable to do this while the barbecue is still
warm. Pour a little oil over it then wipe with a newspaper. Sprinkle
some bicarb and splash over some white vinegar. Then scrub with a
paper towel. Give the hotplate a light oiling once it's cooled, to
prevent rusting. If the stains are really stubborn, try bicarb and
white vinegar then apply sugar and white vinegar to a hot hotplate.

Keep the heat on until the white vinegar completely evaporates.
Then oil the barbecue. Turn it off and wipe down with an old towel.
The reason sugar helps is that it bonds with the dirt and burns. The
oil goes under the sugar and lifts it off.

> **HINT**
>
> **How to remove fat from paving stones**
> What to do will depend on how bad the fat spill is. Begin
> by sprinkling some bicarb over the area, then splash
> some white vinegar on top and rub with a nylon brush.
> Cola also removes fat, but it attracts ants. If the fat has
> penetrated very deeply, use plaster of Paris. Mix
> according to the manufacturer's instructions and apply it
> only to the area affected by the fat. Allow it to set, then
> remove. The fat will pull out with the plaster.

Flyscreens

Flyscreens are a big dirt trap, so it's a good idea to clean them well.
Clean removable ones with the vacuum duster brush attachment.
Vacuum inside and outside the screen and wipe with lemon oil or
lemon peel to discourage spiders. To clean fixed screens on
windows, close the windows, damp the screen with water then
sweep with a soft broom. Rinse with a hose.

Sliding doors

The runners under sliding doors are vulnerable to dirt and rust.
Clear them regularly by vacuuming any dirt between the tracks, but
not if it's wet. Never vacuum anything that's wet because it's
dangerous and could ruin the vacuum cleaner. If you want to get rid
of that squeaky noise, use a graphite puffer and lightly squirt it
along the runner.

THE GARDEN

I love spending time in the garden. And I'm particular about
avoiding toxins. My preference is for natural rather than chemical
solutions. For example:

To keep birds away, hang old CDs in the trees.

To grow moss in the garden place 500 g of moss or lichen in a
blender, add 500 ml of lager and whizz until it resembles a chunky
soup. Spread the mixture over rocks or any ground where you want
moss to grow and don't water it for at least 24 hours. Then water it
very lightly, making sure you don't wash the moss away. To
encourage algae and lichen, paint everything with yoghurt.

Problem:	**Aphids.**
What to use:	**Detergent, cooking oil, water, spray bottle.**
How to apply:	Thoroughly mix 1 tablespoon of washing up liquid and 240 ml of cooking oil. Add 2–3 teaspoons of this mixture to 240 ml of water, put it into a spray bottle and spray your plants.

Problem:	**Snails and slugs getting into pot plants.**
What to use:	**Vaseline.**
How to apply:	Rub some Vaseline each month on the outside of pot plants.

HINT

Move pot plants around regularly so mildew rings don't
form. To remove mould on pots, apply bicarb, then white
vinegar and rub with a nylon brush. Rinse with water,
adding a couple of drops of oil of cloves to the rinse
water to inhibit mould. Leave in the sunshine to dry.

Problem:	**Preventing mildew forming on terracotta pots.**
What to use:	**Unibond PVA, water, oil of cloves.**
How to apply:	To stop mildew forming on terracotta pots, seal with a mixture of 1 part Unibond PVA, 3 parts water and a couple of drops of oil of cloves. It should be the consistency of runny cream. Paint it over the pots and let them dry inside and out.

Garden ponds

If you have a garden pond, stick water hyacinths in it. They clean the water, are easily pulled out with a rake and make a great fertiliser.

Statues

Statues can be large or small. If you want to encourage moss to grow on them, paint them with a mixture of skimmed milk and yoghurt. If you can, use a yoghurt containing acidophilus. To inhibit moss and mould, paint with 1 part oil of cloves to 50 parts water.

> **DID YOU KNOW?** If you want to create an aged look on paths or statues, mould will grow if you add natural yoghurt to the rinse water.

Fences

Clean according to the type of fence it is: most only need to be swept over if they're grotty. Be careful with cutout timber, which can rot if exposed to the weather. Wash with washing up liquid and water applied with a broom.

> Create an everlasting fence post from *Lee's Priceless Recipes*, 1817: Wood can be made to last longer than iron in the ground. Take boiled linseed oil and stir in pulverised charcoal to the consistency of paint. Put a coat of this over the timber. There's not a man who will live to see it rot.

Lawns

A garden always looks tidier if the grass is mown. Long, stray grass going everywhere screams unloved and unkempt. If you're short of time, tidy the area by raking up any big leaves. Then work a stiff garden broom over the grass to tidy it up. It's like giving the lawn a hair-do. I know it sounds strange, but it works. If you have the option, choose trees and plants that don't drop their leaves. Alternatively, don't place your outdoor furniture under trees and plants that do drop their leaves.

Pathways and gates

There are several ways to clean mouldy pathways. Check first by
scrubbing the area with water and a nylon broom just in case it's
accumulated dirt! If it is mould, and there's a garden nearby,
sprinkle bicarb then white vinegar and scrub with a nylon broom. If
there's no garden, add 1 kg of table salt per bucket of warm water
and scrub with a nylon broom. Pool cleaning product, Surex 002
Oxysure, also works, but don't use it if there's run-off to lichen or
ferns.

You can stop gates and hinges squeaking with sewing machine
oil. Add a couple of drops to the noisy hinge. If you get tar on your
clothing, remove it with baby oil. Just rub the baby oil into the tar
until it melts, then add washing up liquid and wash.

Clothes lines

The rotary clothes line is a great invention and sits proudly in many
back gardens. But be aware that if you have galvanised wires they
can rust. The best way to treat them is with rust converter that seals
the metal and forms a hard shiny surface. This needs to be done
only once every three years. Put just a couple of drops on a cloth
and wipe over the wire. Rust converter also seems to inhibit
spiders, which like to live in the anchor points of clothes lines. The
centre mechanism should be wiped with sweet almond oil every six
months. Apply it around the gap in the crown and put the clothes
line up and down so the oil spreads. The great thing about sweet
almond oil is it won't mark your clothes, unlike other lubricants.

Some clothes lines have either copper wires or plastic-coated
wires. Copper produces verdigris (green marks) that stains clothes,
so keep it polished with white vinegar. Clean the wires with white
vinegar before hanging the washing out until the verdigris is gone.

Plastic-coated wires only need to be wiped down every now and then with white vinegar. Just run the cloth along once and you're done!

They're rare, but you may even have a prop line. These have two timber supports at either end, a pivoting head and cotton sash cord strung between. The cord has to be replaced every year because it gathers mould.

PETS

Pet baskets and kennels should be elevated so air can circulate. Put some bricks underneath or build some stilts. Hand wash all pet bedding regularly. To prevent cats coming into the yard, spread Vicks VapoRub onto a few stones. Turn them over to prevent sun and rain damage.

To stop dogs digging in particular area, bury some of their poo in the spot and they'll stay away. To encourage digging, leave bones in a particular spot.

Pets' sleeping areas should be cleaned each week.

Birds

Most birdcages have a tray of sand or sandpaper. When cleaning, slide the contents of the tray into a plastic bag and put it in the bin straightaway. It's okay to put the contents directly into a compost bin, but make sure you bury it or the seed will germinate. Remove the seed and water containers and put the whole cage in a washing up bowl. Run water over the cage, gently giving your budgie a bath at the same time! If you don't have a tub, take it into the shower. Leave the cage to drain and air dry inside or outside.

Cats and dogs

Shake all the bedding thoroughly, then wash in the washing machine. If the bedding is too big, wash it in a washing up bowl with washing powder. If there are fleas, add some mint tea to the washing water. To make mint tea, add 2 teaspoons of dried mint or 3 teaspoons of fresh mint to 240 ml of hot water. Allow the tea to steep for at least 2 minutes then strain it. Also spray the bedding with mint tea. After washing these items, always clean the filters and lint catchers in the washing machine.

HINT

How to wash a cat
Do this regularly if there are people in the house who are allergic to cats. Secure a tea towel over the cat's head and front legs, wrapping it firmly. It won't be able to scratch and the darkness calms it. Clean the back with a pet brush. Then wrap the tea towel over the cat's back legs and wipe the front with a washer going from front to back. Don't use a brush because it irritates them. Use a pet shampoo over the entire cat and pamper the cat afterwards so it has a positive association with washing.

Fish

Clean fish tanks with an old stocking. Just wrap it over your hand to make a mitt and wipe along the inside of the tank. You could also buy some suckerfish, which are known as 'vacuum-cleaner fish', to make cleaning speedier. If you've got an outbreak of algae, check the filter. It may need flushing or replacing. Also check that it is big enough for the tank. Be careful when adding water to a fish tank because sudden changes in temperature can kill the fish. If the water level has dropped and you have to add some more, fill a plastic bag with fresh water, let it sit in the remaining tank water until it becomes the same temperature, then add it slowly to the tank.

DUSTBIN AREA

When I was at primary school, we had a goat that ate the rubbish! With contemporary bins, deter flies, dogs and mosquitoes by adding a couple of drops of lavender oil to a paper towel and wiping it around the edge of the bin. Lemon peel or lemon oil will keep spiders away. To preserve the environment, try to avoid using plastic bags. Instead, put rubbish directly into the bin or wrap it in newspaper.

GARAGE/SHED AND DRIVEWAY

Two of the best ways to clean oil stains and other scum off a driveway or garage floor is to scrub with bicarb and white vinegar or spray it with Surex 002 Oxysure. Leave it until almost dry, then give it a good sweep with a nylon broom before hosing or washing it down. You can also clean oil stains with a carbonated cola drink. If you do, wash the area well or ants will be attracted to it.

When organising a garage or shed, put tools you use most often near the door. There's nothing worse than rummaging around in a space and creating more mess. Have bins for rags and dust cloths and always have a rag bag. The best way to store tools is with a shadow board – it means you can identify your tools at a glance. Other items, such as nails and screws, should be stored in labelled jars. If you have lots of shelving along the walls, fill them with containers. You can use takeaway containers or old ice-cream containers. Reinforce free-standing shelves by placing them back-to-back and bolting them together.

Large power tools should be kept together in a dry area. Don't wrap the cords around the power tools or you'll create kinks. The best way to store electric cords is to hold one end in the space between your thumb and forefinger and wind the cord over your elbow, then back up to your thumb and down again to your elbow until it's coiled. Wind the remaining cord around the top of the coil and plug the two ends together to protect the pins and stop insects taking up residence in the holes. Store the cord inside the cardboard centre from a roll of paper towel.

If the shed is damp, elevate the area by placing an old wooden pallet or bricks on the ground, then add new flooring on top of the pallet or bricks. Keep fuels, chemicals and flammable materials on metal or masonry shelving. Never store them at ground level because they're more likely to come into contact with water that will corrode the cans and cause dangerous spills. Don't place them above eye level either because it is much easier to have accidents when reaching up high. They should also be kept out of direct sunlight. Make sure these materials are in non-corrodible unbreakable containers, are marked clearly, have childproof caps, and are out of reach of children.

Q:
'I've got some rust marks on my garage floor,' says Barbara. 'I think it's from battery acid. What can I do?'

Problem:	**Rust marks on garage floor.**
What to use:	**Bicarb, white vinegar, stiff broom, descaler.**
How to apply:	Clean the surface by sprinkling some bicarb over the area, then sprinkle white vinegar and scrub with a stiff broom. Then use a descaler according to the manufacturer's instructions.

Gardening tools

Along with the lawnmower, strimmer and other equipment, leaf blowers should be stored in a cool, dark place. Protect all blades against rust by wiping them with machine oil applied with a cloth. Wipe the outside of the lawnmower, strimmer, etc, with a mild washing up liquid solution.

Don't throw old hedge clippers away. Pull them apart and recycle them into trowels, a hole digger or to cut grass edges around concrete.

CARS

Clean upholstery and carpet in the car as you would the same fabrics in the house. To add another layer of protection, spray Scotchgard each time you vacuum. Clean plastics with glycerine on a cloth and keep an old pair of tights in the glovebox to clean windows. To protect the heel of your shoe when you're driving, either fix a piece of towel to the mat, or have a dedicated pair of driving shoes.

One of the best ways to cut back on cleaning is to ban people from eating or drinking in the car. If you do spill anything, deal with it as soon as possible. Keep some paper towel and wet wipes in the glove box. Clean any plastics in the car with glycerine applied with a cloth. If someone vomits in the car, the best thing to do is to remove the seat from the car, clean it, apply bicarb, dry it in the sun, then vacuum and return it to the car.

> **HINT**
>
> **If there's a smell in the car**
> Remove the smelly item, then dampen a tea bag in water and add a drop of lavender oil. Find the vents that feed the air conditioning – they are generally located under the dashboard – and leave the tea bag there for a while. If you can't find the vents, leave the tea bag anywhere in the car. The tea works because it kills dust mites and mildew, and the lavender particles are small enough to get into the air conditioning and leave a fresh smell. Some car manufacturers add fragrance to their air conditioning: now you can do it yourself!

Problem: Scratches on the dashboard or on plastic surfaces.
What to use: Glycerine, cloth.
How to apply: Add 1 part glycerine to 5 parts warm water then wipe over the surface with a cloth. Glycerine will also give the surface a good sheen.

Problem: Sticky adhesive on car window.
What to use: Cling film, washing up liquid.
How to apply: Tear off a piece of cling film larger than the size of the adhesive. Mix 1 part washing up liquid and 20 parts water and spray on the cling film then place this over the sticker. Leave it for about 5 minutes or until the adhesive comes loose. Then peel off the cling wrap. The adhesive will peel off too.

Q:

'I've got the smell of mould in my car,' says Pete.
'I think the carpet must have got wet at some
stage. What do you suggest?'

Problem:	**Mould smell in car.**
What to use:	**Oil of cloves.**
How to apply:	The smell comes from the bacteria and mould and the best way to fix it is with sunshine. If possible, take the carpet out of the car and leave it in the sun. If you can't, park the car on a funny angle or slope and leave the doors open so sun gets in. Or wipe the carpet with a little oil of cloves.

CARAVANS AND BOATS

Some caravans and boats could be considered houses in their own
right. I won't include a comprehensive guide to their upkeep but
here are a couple of real-life problems.

Q:

'I've got a pop-top caravan and the nylon zips
have become stuck,' says Rick.

Problem:	**Sticky nylon zips.**
What to use:	**Glycerine/lead pencil or graphite.**
How to apply:	Wipe the zipper with glycerine. For metal zips, use a lead pencil or graphite.

Q: Val's husband and son are going away for a boys'
holiday in their caravan. But they've left her with the
job of fixing the scratches on the polycarbonate
dome skylight. 'We were advised to clean them
with a particular product, but it scratched them. Are
there any solutions?'

Problem:	**Scratches in polycarbonate.**
What to use:	**Ceramicoat.**
How to apply:	It's very difficult to take scratches out. One option is to try a product called Ceramicoat. Do a test patch first, and, if it works, reglaze the dome in very thin coats. Spray one coat, leave it for 5 minutes, spray another coat and then leave for 24 hours. Repeat if necessary. To prevent scratching, use car wax, but make sure it doesn't have a cutting compound.

Q: 'We've got a boat and the inside is covered with a
white nylon carpet,' says Lynn, 'but it's starting to
stain black and mildewy. What can we do? It's
really hard to put new carpet in a boat!'

Problem:	**Mildew in boat carpet.**
What to use:	**Surex 002 Oxysure, bucket, water.**
How to apply:	Because the carpet is nylon, wash it with diluted Surex.

SWIMMING POOL

If it's hot and you've got a pool, everyone wants to be your friend.
But, despite the range of accessories, cleaning a pool can be

painstaking. If it's all a bit too much for you, hire a professional pool cleaner.

There are a few things that need regular maintenance. Firstly, make sure the water level is high enough. Maintaining the right pH level is also important. You should already have a testing kit but, if you don't, you can buy them. Be aware that chlorine is affected by the sun. The more sunny days there are, the more chlorine you'll need to use. If you don't like chlorine because it's toxic, try Surex 002 Oxysure.

Skim the top of the pool regularly to collect leaves so they don't clog the filter. In fact, don't leave anything in the pool because it could get caught in the filter.

Clean the tiles with Gumption and a stiff brush. Create traction on slate surrounds by mixing 1 part Surex 002 Oxysure, 20 parts water and 225 g of sand.

Keep sunscreen and spare towels near the pool. That way you won't have wet feet tramping through the house.

 'My swimming pool has a stain all around the edge,' reports John. 'The walls are made of pebble-crete.'

Problem:	**Stain around swimming pool.**
What to use:	**Stiff brush, Gumption.**
How to apply:	It's painstaking, but it works. Get a stiff brush, put some Gumption on it and scrub the stain off bit by bit.

SPAS AND SAUNAS

Bacteria can thrive in spas. Backflush with white vinegar after every second use and change the water regularly. Maintain the right chemical level, which is generally higher than that for swimming pools. Check the manufacturer's instruction. If the spa has a wooden surround, add a couple of drops of oil of cloves to the rinse water to keep mildew at bay.

Maintain the heating and filter units of a sauna by cleaning regularly according to the manufacturer's instructions. Add a few drops of oil or cloves to keep mildew away and add your favourite herbs to the hot stones for a super sauna.

CHAPTER 9:
The Laundry

Your laundry may be a whole room in the house or an area tucked behind a cupboard door in the bathroom. The contents are generally the same wherever your laundry is situated – a washing machine, dryer and sink. It's important that you learn how to look after your laundry white goods and the items that go into them: all will last longer if handled with care!

How good is the washing machine? It's so much quicker than the days of using the copper, washing board and lots of elbow grease. You simply throw the dirty clothes in the machine, add a bit of washing powder, set the cycle and about half an hour later, the clothes are all clean. Imagine life without it! But how do you work out which washing powder is the best? And what's the best way to hang your washing?

The dryer is another device that has been designed to make our lives easier. Many people opt to use the dryer because they don't have a clothes line or can't be bothered hanging out the washing. But keep this in mind: sunshine is a great antibacterial!

ASSEMBLE THE CLEAN KIT

bicarb – cleaning agent
broom – to sweep the floor and other surfaces
cloth – to wipe surfaces
clutter bucket – to transport displaced items
old toothbrush – to access tight corners
rubber gloves – to protect your hands
scrubbing brush – to scrub with
white vinegar – cleaning agent

ASSEMBLE THE WASHING KIT

bar of soap
bicarb
buckets
cheap bottle of shampoo and conditioner
clothes basket
good-quality washing powder or liquid
oil of cloves
scrubbing brush
table salt
Vanish
Vanish Oxi Action
white vinegar

CLEANING SPECIFIC TO THE LAUNDRY

Clear anything that doesn't belong in the laundry by placing it in the clutter bucket. Wipe the outside of the washing machine and dryer with a cloth that's been wrung out in water. If the washing machine and dryer are very dirty, add white vinegar to the cloth. Wipe any benches or other surfaces in the laundry by sprinkling over a little bicarb, then spraying white vinegar on top and wiping with a cloth. Wipe over the sink with a little bicarb and white vinegar and mop the floor with an old T-shirt that's been dampened in white vinegar and secured around the broom head with an elastic band.

Never store washing powder or washing liquid on the laundry window sill because they're affected by light and will make a mess. Instead, keep your cleaning items on an enclosed shelf. If they're stored under the sink, protect them from damp by storing them in a plastic container.

Q: 'I've got the worst problem,' reports Coral. 'Pigeons have decided to roost in the ceiling above my laundry and have pooped all over the concrete floor. I've cleaned away as much as I can but there's still white staining. What can I do?'

Problem: Pigeon poo on concrete floor.

What to use: Bicarb, white vinegar, nylon broom.

How to apply: Sprinkle some bicarb over the floor as though you're dusting icing sugar on a cake. Then sprinkle some white vinegar over the top. While it's fizzing, scrub with a nylon broom. Then rinse with water. And, if you want to deter pigeons, or indeed any kind of bird, buy a rubber snake around 20 cm long and place it where they can see it. They'll stay away! You could also cover the holes in the roof with chicken wire.

WASHING

I think the washing machine is one of the best inventions. I love throwing dirty things in and, like magic, getting clean things out. Here are my general principles for washing clothes:

❑ Use the least amount of chemical and heat to clean. This helps clothes to last longer. Wash whites and colours

separately. You're less likely to get that grey look if you
further separate colours into pale blues and greens, put
darker blues and greys together, and wash blacks, browns
and reds together. I make a pile of clothes in each of these
colour ranges and wait until there's a full load. Have a
minimum of three washing baskets: four is adequate; five is
optimum. Differentiate each basket either by its shape or
colour. Have one basket for whites; another for colourfast
clothes; another for dark items; another for sheets, towels
and light-coloured tea towels and another for hand
washing. I also have a separate basket for reds! When a
basket is full, it's time to wash no matter which day or night
of the week it is. If space is limited, place your washing in
colour-coded plastic crates and stack them vertically.

❑ Always make sure the lint filters in the dryer and washing
machine are clean. You'll get a better result and it's safer.

❑ Don't overpack the washing machine or dryer. Pack
clothes loosely so that the machine has a chance to
agitate them. Never fill more than half of the dryer space
with damp clothes.

❑ The best fabric softener is 60 g of bicarb added to the
washing powder, then add 120 ml of white vinegar to the
rinse cycle.

❑ Buy products according to quality rather than cost.
A suggested range includes:
Good quality washing powder or liquid
Antibacterial agent
Woolwash with eucalyptus or cheap shampoo
Box pure soap flakes
Bottle of cheap hair conditioner

❑ Choose soap powder based on its oxygenated properties
and enzyme content. When soap powder comes into

contact with water, it creates a chemical reaction and effer-
vesces, allowing bubbles of oxygen to attack stains.
Enzymes attack proteins and fats. Cheaper powders tend to
have bleaching agents and are not as good for your clothes.

❏ Liquid soap is usually better than powder because fewer
particles are left on your clothes. This does vary according
to the washing machine with some front loaders
performing better with powder.

❏ If you suffer from skin allergies, test the washing powder
on your skin before using it on your clothes.

❏ If someone in the house has a cold, add 60 ml of lemon
juice or 60 ml of white vinegar to the rinse water to
remove bacteria.

❏ Add 60 ml of white vinegar to the rinse water if your baby
has sensitive skin.

HINT

Hot versus cold water
Only use hot water if you have really soiled clothes,
otherwise it's not necessary, but be aware that hot water
puts more pressure on the fibres of your clothes. If the
item has normal soiling, use the warm setting. I tend to
use the warm setting with a cold rinse. Never use hot
water on delicates. Nylons should only be washed in cold
water. If in doubt, consult the washing labels on your
clothes. There should be a temperature guide.

HINT

Close zips before washing so they don't catch on other
clothes – it's also better for the hang of the clothes. Velcro
strips should be stuck together and the clothes placed
inside a pillowcase or washing bag, which is available at
the supermarket, before being washed. To make Velcro
stick better, wet both the fluffy and spiky sides and comb
with a nit comb.

Before putting washing in the machine, check all pockets. There's nothing worse than a tissue going through the wash and leaving white fluff on everything. If you do get a rogue tissue in your wash, there are two things to clean: the interior of the washing machine and the contents of the wash. To remove fluff from the washing machine, put your hand inside the toe of a pair of pantyhose and wipe over the drum. To remove fluff from your clothes, put on a pair of disposable rubber gloves, wash with a cake of bathroom soap and water and shake dry. Stroke over the linty fabric and the lint will attach to the rubber gloves.

Spot cleaning

Dampen the stain with water first. Mix Vanish Oxi Action and water to form a paste to the consistency of peanut butter. Leave the paste on the stain for 5–15 minutes and, unless it's hand wash only, put the item through the washing machine.

Starches

The best starch is rice water. Next time you're cooking rice, keep the water after it's boiled. There are two ways of using it. You can either dilute it 1 to 1 with water and put it in a spray bottle ready to apply when you're ironing or you can add it to the rinse water in the washing machine.

REMOVING STAINS ON FABRIC

To find out how to remove stains from clothing see Chapter 7.
Below is a kind of ready reference or quick guide to stain removal
from fabrics.

Beer (including   Paint a paste of Napisan Oxygen on the stain and
dark beer)   leave for 15 minutes. Then wash normally.

Beetroot   Treat with glycerine before washing normally.

Bird droppings   Wash fabric normally.

Blood   Wash fresh bloodstains through the washing
machine on the cold setting. If you can't, rub in
cornflour and water. For old bloodstains, use cold
water and soap.

Chewing gum   Harden the gum with ice and cut as much off as
possible with scissors or a blade.

Chocolate   First clean with soap and cold water. Then clean
with soap and hot water.

Coffee or tea   For fresh stains, use glycerine applied with a cotton
wool ball, then wash in washing powder. For old
stains, use glycerine, then dry-cleaning fluid and
washing up liquid.

Egg yolk   Use soap and cold water first, then washing powder
and warm water.

Fruit juice   Use washing up liquid and sunshine. For stone fruits and fruits with a high tannin, treat the stain with glycerine first.

Grease and oil   Detergent suds. For heavy staining, soak in baby oil first.

Ink or ballpoint pen   Rotten milk. Use glycerine first on red ink.

Milk   Wash normally on cold cycle.

Mud   For black mud, wash in the washing machine using a cold wash.

Rust   Use descaler or lemon juice and salt.

Soft drinks   Treat as though it's a fruit stain because soft drink colourings are made of vegetable dyes.

Sweat   Make a paste of Vanish Oxi Action and water and leave on the stain for 15 minutes before washing normally.

Urine   Wash in washing powder and dry in sunshine.

Vomit   Washing powder, sunshine or Vanish, washing machine and dryer.

Wax   Ice.

Wine   New red wine – white vinegar.
Old red wine – glycerine, bicarb and washing up liquid.
White wine – white vinegar.

To soften towels, mix 30 g of bicarb with the washing powder and add 60 ml of white vinegar to the rinse water. For really dirty towels, soak them overnight in a solution of 480 ml of white vinegar to a bucket of water. Then wash them normally. You'll find that they're much softer and the fibres won't be prickly any more.

If you want to anti-static your underwear, petticoats, bras and nylon knits, add a small quantity of hair conditioner to the rinse water when you're washing them.

When washing silk, add 1 teaspoon of salt or white vinegar to the rinse water. This will help keep the silk soft and prevent the colour from running.

CLEANING THE WASHING MACHINE

Clean the inside of the washing machine with bicarb and white vinegar using the two-sponge technique. It's important to do this each week to stop washing powder building up inside the machine. If there are smells, check the pipes. Pipes are really easy and inexpensive to replace. Repairing them will add to the life of your washing machine and stop solid matter getting from the pipes into the bearings. Check the lint catcher in both the washing machine and dryer. Always check the bottom of the washing machine drum in case buttons have come loose or coins have fallen from pockets. Create a spot in the laundry for all these bits and pieces. I have a plastic basket that I leave on the window sill. Use whatever works for you.

Q: 'My washing machine is 20 years old,' reports Wendy. 'It's still working remarkably well, but has a mildewy smell. Is there a solution?'

Problem:	Mildew smell in washing machine.
What to use:	New hose/bicarb, white vinegar.
How to apply:	The smell could be from a variety of sources. Check the netting sections in the lint catchers first. The smell could also come from the hose, which is very easy to change. Another source could be the joints in the plumbing. If it's from the machine bowl, when it's dry, wipe it with bicarb and white vinegar. If the smell persists, run the washing machine on empty with 115 g of bicarb and add 480 ml of white vinegar during the rinse cycle.

Q: 'I've got black stuff in my washing machine,' says Ngaire. 'What should I do?'

Problem:	Black stuff in washing machine.
What to use:	Bicarb, white vinegar/replace seals.
How to apply:	Add 60 g of bicarb to hot washing water. Then add 120 ml or white vinegar to the rinse water. If this doesn't work, replace the seals on your washing machine.

DID YOU KNOW? The washing machine has a lint catcher. Your washing will be cleaner if the lint catcher is cleared regularly. In front loaders it is located near the door or at the back of the machine. In a top loader, it's located either on top of the agitator or in a little bag on the side of the drum in the machine. Consult the instructions if you're not sure where yours is. Some modern machines have an automatic clearer so it doesn't need to be cleaned. If your lint catcher is on top of the agitator, put on rubber gloves and unscrew the top. It may be difficult to undo if you haven't cleaned it for a while. If this is the case, smear the joint with a little sweet almond oil. Clear any gunk and return the lint catcher to its spot. If you have a bag, clean it out and flush with water until it's clear, then return.

HAND WASHING

Hand wash in a sink or bucket. You can also use the hand wash setting on the washing machine, though I prefer not to. Only ever wash delicates or wool in blood-heat water. To test for blood heat, sprinkle a few drops of water on the inside of your wrist. If you can't feel the water – that is, if it's the same temperature as your wrist – it's blood heat.

HANGING OUT THE WASHING

These days, we're more likely to put clothes in the dryer but it means missing out on one of the best antibacterial cleaners around – the sun. The sun also adds fragrance to your clothes so I suggest making the effort to hang your clothes on the line. The first rule of hanging out the washing is that everyone hates ironing – so hang it well!

When you hang out your washing, hang each item by the strongest section of the garment and always place pegs in unobtrusive spots. Trousers and skirts should be hung from the waistband. Shirts should be hung from the tails and pegged on the side seams. Shirts can also be put on a coathanger with a plastic shopping bag over the wire to prevent rusting.

Woollens are best dried lying flat on a white towel (to avoid colour transference). If you have to hang something woollen, put an old stocking through the sleeves and peg the stocking to the line.

Towels should be hung over the line in half so that the edges sit against each other. They'll take longer to dry, but will be fluffier. Hang anything with a nap or fluff with the fluff surfaces facing each other. This works particularly well with towels that have a velvety finish on one side and a normal finish on the other. Drape the towel in half over the line with the 'velvet' side on the inside. They'll take longer to dry but it's worth it when one side is fluffy and soft.

Use plastic bags to hang delicates on the clothes line. Place the plastic bag over the line and drape the delicates over the bag, then wrap the bag back over the delicates and peg.

Never hang silk on a windy day because the fibres tangle and are difficult to smooth out.

You're less likely to get holes if you hang socks by the tops rather than the toes. Old netted bags from the fruit shop make great peg bags because water drains through them. Wrap the netted bag around a coathanger that has been opened into a circle. The hook makes it easy to hang.

Bird poo can bleach your clothes because it's high in lime. To stop birds hovering over your clothes line and potentially soiling your clothes, tie some coloured ribbons to the line and allow them to flutter. You could also hang some old CDs on the line. Birds don't like sharp movements. Never leave pegs on the washing line because they deteriorate.

TUMBLE DRYING

Drying in the sun is preferable, but I know that's not always an option. Before using your dryer, make sure you clean the lint catcher. To cut back on ironing, fold your clothes as soon as they come out of the dryer. If you're in a hurry and need to speed up the drying process, put a dry tea towel in with your clothes. It will absorb moisture.

To get rid of static, wash and dry synthetics separately from clothes made of natural fibres. Never overdry synthetic fibres. Remove them from the dryer slightly damp and hang to dry naturally either on a clothes line or on hangers.

Most people know that the dryer has a lint catcher and must be cleared before each use. Some dryers also have a water condenser which should also be checked and emptied each time before drying. I clean the inside of the dryer with an old pair of tights in case anything, such as plastics, have wiped against the drum.

If you use your dryer often, the area around it, including the wall, will accumulate lint. The best way to clear it is with a vacuum cleaner, using the brush attachment.

> **HINT**
>
> Be careful using the dryer with clothes that have large metal attachments. Either remove the metal or turn the item inside out so that the metal doesn't come into contact with the drum and damage it.

IRONING

Many years ago when my eldest daughter was a baby, I used to iron professionally. One of the main rules of good ironing is to go with the grain. Find out which way the grain runs by holding the fabric and pulling it. If it's taut, you're on the grain. If you have stretch, you're not on the grain.

I like to iron clothes while they're slightly damp because it speeds up the process. Have some water in a spray pack and squirt a mist over the clothes before running the iron over them. I also like to set the iron on low temperatures and use lots of steam.

When you're ironing wool, use a damp white linen tea towel over the top. Rest and press the iron but don't leave it in the one spot for too long.

Use spray starches sparingly because they can damage your clothes and make your floors slippery.

I like to protect buttons on shirts by making a cardboard cutout like a thick letter 'c' and placing this under the button. Slide the iron between the shirt and the cardboard. I have my 'c' tied to the iron with a piece of elastic.

To sharpen pleats when ironing, lay the garment over the end of the ironing board and, using glass-headed or steel-headed pins, pin the pleats into position on the ironing board. Hold the pleat taut at both ends. Put a damp cloth over the pleat and run the iron gently up and down. For sharp, long-lasting creases, rub soap down the inside of the crease before you iron the garment. This will stop your trousers getting baggy knees!

The legs of old pyjamas make great ironing-board covers. Secure them with safety pins underneath the board.

Speed up the ironing process by putting a sheet of aluminium foil under the ironing board cover.

Clean an iron when it's cold with bicarb and white vinegar. Just make sure you clean it all off properly with water before using it again. To clean the sticky build-up on the bottom of an iron, get a piece of rough blotting paper, preferably white, and rub the hot iron backwards and forwards over it until no more marks come off.

Q: 'Is there any way to unpleat permanent pleating?'

Problem: Unpleating permanent pleating.
What to use: Steam from the iron.
How to apply: The effectiveness of this technique will depend on whether the fabric is natural or synthetic. For natural fabrics, remove the pleat using lots of steam from the iron. It's very difficult to get pleats out of synthetic fabrics because they have a memory and return to their original pleats.

Q: 'What's the best way to iron a damask tablecloth?' asks Sue.

Problem: Ironing damask.
What to use: Old blanket, iron.
How to apply: Make sure the ironing board has thick padding. An old folded blanket will do. Slightly dampen the tablecloth then iron with the warp of the fabric. The warp goes down the fabric; the weft goes across the fabric.

If you accidentally drop a hot iron on the carpet

If the scorch mark is light and the carpet is colourfast, cut a cloth to the size of the burn, dip it in 3 per cent hydrogen peroxide solution and lay it over the mark for 2 minutes. Rinse with a damp cloth. If the burn is very bad, clip the surface of the wool with scissors or patch it. To patch the carpet, cut around the damaged part of the carpet into a manageable shape with a Stanley knife. Find a piece of the carpet (perhaps some leftover or cut from somewhere little seen, such as from inside the cupboard) a little larger than the stained area. Make sure the pattern is in the same direction. Then make a paper template of the stained area and transfer this to the piece of patch carpet. Cut the patch around the template with a sharp knife. You'll need some carpet tape, which is available from carpet manufacturers, dealers and some hardware shops. Attach the tape under the edges of the damaged carpet so that the adhesive side is facing upward. Make sure that half of the tape is under the old carpet and the other half is exposed in the hole. Then press the patch carpet into the hole, sticking it to the exposed half of the tape. Brush the carpet in both directions until the fibres line up on the edges. Stand on the area for 5 minutes to make sure it sticks well. Then place a book on top of the patch for 24 hours.

> **HINT**
>
> **Ironing without an iron**
> To stiffen or smooth tulle, nylon and other fabrics you can't iron, put 1 tablespoon of uncoloured pure soap flakes into a spray bottle and mix with 1 litre of water. Shake the mixture until the soap flakes have completely dissolved and then spray the fabric. Pull the fabric straight and dry it with a hairdryer. Don't hold the hairdryer too close or the heat will melt the fabric. The mixture stiffens and irons at the same time.

FOLDING

The general principle for folding is to have as few folds as possible. Size up the space you have available and then work out the least number of folds for the greatest surface area of the shelf or drawer. Never put a fold down the front of a garment.

Fold socks by matching the tops together and folding three edges over you hand and the other edge over itself. Then remove your hand. Another way is to lay the socks flat, fold them at the heels and pull the top edge over your hand. Then remove your hand.

Fold a tea towel in six squares. Fold towels in half depending on the size of the shelf. You can also fold towels in half and then roll them up. This helps them to stay fluffy and looks good.

To prevent creasing in good tablecloths, place a piece of acid-free paper along the middle line.

LAUNDRY – FREQUENTLY ASKED QUESTIONS

What can you do if you've got a mountain of ironing?

Iron flat things first, such as tablecloths and tea towels, because they're easy, or iron the things you hate most, then reward yourself. As soon as you have a bundle of items, put them away: it's a good visual reward. Iron shirts last because they have to be hung up. Watch TV, listen to your favourite music or do what a women I know did; set up an ironing board across a treadmill and walk while you iron!

How do you unshrink a shrunken jumper?

For dark-coloured jumpers, fill a nappy bucket with blood-heat water and add 2 tablespoons of Fuller's earth. For light-coloured jumpers, add 4 tablespoons of Fuller's earth. Put the jumper in and gently agitate it with your hands until it's thoroughly wet. Let it sit for 10–15 minutes and then rinse completely in blood-heat water. Don't leave it for longer than this or it will bleach. Don't wring out the jumper but gently squeeze out as much water as possible. Then place the jumper on a towel in a shady spot and dry it flat. Gently stretch it back into shape as it's drying. To make the stretch more even, use two wide-toothed combs on either side of the jumper and stretch with the combs as it's drying. It's not as effective but you could also use 2 tablespoons of Epsom salts, instead of Fuller's earth added to a bucket of blood-heat water.

What's the best way to dry leather shoes?

Dust inside each shoe with bicarb and pack with newspaper or paper towel. The newspaper or paper towel will absorb the moisture out of the leather so it retains more of its suppleness. It will allow the shoes to dry back into shape without going stiff. Then polish with shoe polish.

DID YOU KNOW? Many cloth shoes can be cleaned in the washing machine. Secure them in an old pillowcase before washing. The pillowcase protects the washing machine. Dry in the sunshine not the dryer.

How should I clean trainers?

Clean leather trainers with Vaseline. Clean cloth trainers by placing them in a pillowcase and washing in the machine. If you have a mixture of the two, clean the cloth part with white vinegar on a toothbrush and wipe Vaseline over the leather sections.

If you suffer from athlete's foot, wipe tea tree oil on the affected area and rub it inside your shoes.

How should you clean delicates?

Protect delicates by placing them in a mesh wash bag. This stops them from being flung around the machine and getting damaged. It also prevents underwire bras from getting caught in the washing machine, which can be expensive to fix.

How long should you soak clothes?

You'd think that the longer you soak your clothes, the more dirt is removed, but this is not actually the case. Some items need soaking overnight. Others, such as delicates, should be soaked for only half an hour. Never soak woollens for more than 20 minutes because the fibres shrink when the water cools.

For clothes that have been soaked and rinsed, speed their drying by putting them in the washing machine and using just the spin cycle. This will remove a lot of the water.

Should you turn clothes inside out?

Anything that has artwork on it, a transfer or design should be turned inside out before washing. Imagine the transfer on your favourite T-shirt hitting the metal drum of the washing machine as it washes. It can't be good for it. Anything that has a nap, such as velveteen, should be turned inside out to wash. Socks should be turned the right way out, that is, the way you wear them. They tend to be dirtier on the outside than the inside. Protect the colour of jeans by turning them inside out. Any clothes made from corduroy or velvet should also be turned inside out.

Liquid versus powder?

I prefer liquid because it's less abrasive and has less soap build-up.
If you can't get liquid, dissolve the powder in water before adding it
to your wash. Check the instructions for front loaders as some
stipulate using powder only. I use bicarb and white vinegar as a
fabric softener for towels and sheets. I never use commercial ones
because they irritate my skin. Wear rubber gloves when working
with enzyme products because they can damage your skin.

Wash woollens in shampoo and rinse them in hair conditioner to keep them soft. Use 1 cap per bucket of water
and always use blood-heat water.

How do you prevent colour from running?

Many clothes from India and Asia aren't colourfast. Check the label
first. If you're not sure, test an inconspicuous part of the garment.
To test for colourfastness, wring a cloth out in white vinegar, place
it over the garment and iron it. Colour will transfer to the cloth if it's
not colourfast. Always be extra careful with red clothes.

To stop colours running, either hand wash or machine
wash them in blood-heat water with table salt and
washing powder. Use 225 g of salt and 1 tablespoon of
washing powder per nappy bucket of blood-heat water.

What do I do if I've left damp clothes in the washing machine?

It's okay to leave damp washing in the machine for up to 12 hours before it gets that musty smell. If your clothes do smell musty, add 25 g of bicarb to the washing water and 60 ml of white vinegar to the rinse water.

> **DID YOU KNOW?** Adding a little lemon juice to the rinse water whitens clothes.

Q: 'My shirts have ink stains all over them, particularly in the top pockets,' says Tony. 'Is there a solution?'

Problem:	Biro stains on shirt.
What to use:	Rotten milk.
How to apply:	One of the best ways to remove biro stains is with rotten milk. Place some full cream milk in the sun until it forms solids. Then apply the solids to the stain until the ink starts to drift up through the milk solids. Then wash normally.

What should I do if I spill bleach on my clothes?

Match the colour with fabric paint. If you can't get the exact colour, mix the paints until you get a match. With a sable paintbrush, paint over the bleached area and feather it into the unbleached area. When it's dry, iron the back of the garment to make it colourfast.

> If you do all your washing in one day, make sure the first
> loads contain the heaviest items, such as towels, jeans or
> jumpers. The reason – they take longer to dry!

How do I get rid of these strange stains?

To remove fake tan, treat it as a tannin and an oil stain. Wipe with glycerine first, then use washing-up liquid and sponge out.

To remove sun block, use washing-up liquid and water.

To remove liquid found in Fluorescent Glo-sticks, soak the item in 225 g of table salt to a bucket of cold water for about 20 minutes. Then freeze the item. Once it's frozen, wash normally.

> To remove perspiration stains, make a paste of Vanish
> powder and water. You could also mix 1 tablespoon of
> cream of tartare, 3 aspirin tablets and warm water. Paint
> on the stain, leave for 20 minutes, then wash with warm
> water.

What should you do about grass stains?

A natural way of removing grass stains is to use 1 part egg white and 1 part glycerine, which forms a soapy paste. Both have to be the same temperature when mixed, so leave the eggs out of the fridge. Leave the paste on the stain for one day then wash in blood-heat water. It's how cricket whites used to be cleaned.

Index